# JOHN AND BETTY
# STAM

## Missionary Martyrs

Vance Christie

BARBOUR
PUBLISHING, INC.
Uhrichsville, Ohio

## Other books in the "Heroes of the Faith" series:

*Brother Andrew*
*Gladys Aylward*
*Dietrich Bonhoeffer*
*William and Catherine Booth*
*John Bunyan*
*William Carey*
*Amy Carmichael*
*George Washington Carver*
*Fanny Crosby*
*Frederick Douglass*
*Jonathan Edwards*
*Jim Elliot*
*Charles Finney*
*Billy Graham*
*C. S. Lewis*
*Eric Liddell*
*David Livingstone*
*Martin Luther*
*D. L. Moody*

*Samuel Morris*
*George Müller*
*Watchman Nee*
*John Newton*
*Florence Nightingale*
*Luis Palau*
*Francis and Edith Schaeffer*
*Charles Sheldon*
*Mary Slessor*
*Charles Spurgeon*
*Billy Sunday*
*Hudson Taylor*
*William Tyndale*
*Corrie ten Boom*
*Mother Teresa*
*Sojourner Truth*
*John Wesley*
*George Whitefield*

© 2000 by Barbour Publishing, Inc.

ISBN 1-57748-834-2

Published by Barbour Publishing, Inc., P.O. Box 719, Uhrichsville, OH 44683
http://www.barbourbooks.com

Cover illustration © Dick Bobnick.

ecpa Member of the
Evangelical Christian
Publishers Association

Printed in the United States of America.

# JOHN AND BETTY
# STAM

# *Dedication*

To my parents, George and Phyllis Christie,
who taught me the way of the Lord
by exhortation and example,
and who continue to bless me
by their prayers and encouragement

# *one*

The fateful day began with deceptive normalcy at John and Betty Stam's missionary residence in Tsingteh, China. Both the wood-burning stoves had been lit and were starting to heat up nicely, helping to lessen the chill that gripped the large old house that cold, early December morning. The Stams, along with the six Chinese who lived with them in the house, had already eaten breakfast.

John hoped to study and get some correspondence done that morning. Betty was preparing to give their three-month-old baby, Helen Priscilla, a bath, with some assistance from the amah Mei Tsong-fuh. The cook, Li Ming-chin, busied himself in the kitchen. His wife, mother, and two children similarly had begun their various daily activities.

John and Betty had been in Tsingteh for just two weeks. They had come there under the auspices of the China Inland Mission (CIM) to oversee the infant Christian work that had been established in the southern portion of Anhwei Province. There were very few Christians in the area, but the Stams were thrilled at the prospect of carrying out pioneer evangelistic work to help bring the Gospel to that needy part of China.

For John and Betty this was a longtime dream come true. Several years earlier they had both dedicated their lives to vocational Christian service. While students at Moody Bible Institute, they separately concluded that the Lord would have them serve Him in China. God had not only brought them to China (Betty first, then John a year later), but also had allowed them to be joined as husband and wife there.

They had thoroughly enjoyed their first year of marriage and serving the Lord together, the birth of their beautiful daughter having been the crowning joy of that year. While they realized that there would sometimes be difficult challenges, they looked forward, God willing, to having many more years of happy missionary service together as a family.

Just after eight that morning a messenger sent by the town magistrate arrived at the Stams' home. "The magistrate told me to call at your house," he explained to John, "to notify you and your wife that Communist soldiers were at Yang Chi, fifty or sixty li away, last night. You must be on your guard, and if the rumors become alarming, you must leave."[1]

John, knowing that a li equaled about one-third of a mile, sought to reassure the man. He reached out a hand and patted the messenger's shoulder, saying, "Don't be alarmed, they won't come to this small place. But thank you for coming to tell me."

Just weeks earlier John and a fellow missionary had

conducted a careful investigation of the region to determine the advisability of bringing his family to Tsingteh to begin mission work there. "Due to the drought and shortage of food, there has been an increase of bandit activity in the area," local magistrates candidly informed the missionaries. "But you need not fear a Communist offensive. Many government troops have been brought into the southern half of our province to discourage a Communist incursion here. Government forces are only a short distance away if such a threat develops. And if any trouble does arise, we will be personally responsible for your family's protection."

Having received these assurances, and knowing that conditions in many parts of China were never totally safe for missionaries, John and the CIM officials concluded that it would be appropriate for him and his family to settle in Tsingteh. During the two weeks they had lived in the town, he had heard some talk about the threat of a Communist attack, but that was generally thought to be little more than worrisome gossip.

After the messenger left, John was approached by Li. Deep concern registered on the cook's face and in his voice. "Since the magistrate has sent this man to warn you and since the Reds are not so far away, you and your family should go," Li said. When he saw that John looked unconvinced, he continued. "The Reds are not like local bandits. Their number is large and they are not afraid of a local garrison. Besides, their movements are very uncertain. They're here today and there tomorrow."

"We'll wait awhile and see," John responded calmly. "This afternoon a pastor is coming from the neighboring province, and we shall see what news he brings."

About an hour later Li's mother left the Stams' house

9

and went out on the street to have a pair of shoes mended. Suddenly a man who had been sent out as a scout into the countryside by the magistrate came running down the street. Covered with sweat, the man shouted to people as he passed, "It's bad! Quick! The Reds will soon be here! They're only a little over ten li away."

He went directly to the magistrate's office at the local yamen. Upon hearing the news, Magistrate Peng ordered the city gates to be closed at once. Seeing all this, Li's mother hastened back to the Stam home and reported the happenings to her son. He went to the door and saw people running in all directions.

With fear welling in his heart, Li said to John, "The Red soldiers are certainly near or the people wouldn't be running like this."

"Surely they wouldn't travel so fast—nearly twenty miles in one night. But I'll go out and see what I can learn for myself."

Mei began to tremble with fright. She went into the room where Betty was still caring for Helen. "You must finish with the baby quickly," she said. "We must leave. It is very bad outside."

Betty smiled at her and said quietly, "Don't be afraid, Mei. We trust in God. There is nothing to fear."

A short while later John returned and Li urgently inquired, "How about it, Mr. Stam? Shouldn't we go?"

"I spoke to a man down the street just now," the missionary reported, "and he says that the Red soldiers are at Chiki, seventy li south of here."

"At Chiki?!" Li exclaimed incredulously, hardly able to restrain his anxiety any longer. "When they're actually within ten li of us! Please, Mr. Stam, let me go and order chairs."

John consented and Li hastened away to the chair hong, or warehouse, to hire a pair of chairs and two baggage carriers. After the servant left, John said to Betty, "Why don't you gather a few essential items from our trunks into a bundle just in case we do need to leave here for a few days. I'll get some canned milk and other food items from the kitchen."

Just then a uniformed soldier from the magistrate's yamen came to the house and told John, "You must go. The Red soldiers will soon be in the city."

"We're preparing our things now to go," he responded. It was by then after 10:00 A.M.

Li returned with the chair men who stated that they wanted thirty-two dollars to transport the Stams and their belongings. John immediately agreed to their price.

"The big west gate is still open," the carriers said. "We can go out that way. The Red soldiers are coming from the east."

Presently one of the magistrate's personal bodyguards arrived at the Stams' home. "They are already almost here," the bodyguard announced. "You must leave at once."

"But we will have to go look for chairs," the carriers then revealed. "All the chairs at the hong were already hired."

"Then go at once to find chairs!" Li commanded with obvious agitation in his voice. "Come back here and wait outside."

At that moment, however, rifle shots rang out from the city wall and were promptly answered by reporting fire from outside the town. That could only mean the local militia was exchanging fire with Communist troops. Immediately all but one of the carriers fled.

The militia, numbering less than one hundred men,

11

was no match for the Communist force of over two thousand soldiers. Militia members tore off their uniforms and deserted their posts. Magistrate Peng, who had been out in the streets directing the feeble resistance effort, quickly disguised himself as a farmer and was able to slip out of the city undetected.

The Communists used four ladders to scale the city's accessible eastern wall, then the first soldiers into Tsingteh threw open the east gate to provide the bulk of the force easy entrance into the city. Within minutes Red soldiers had the town completely surrounded on both the outside and inside of its walls, cutting off all possible escape routes.

The missionary residence was located not far from the city's east gate. When the firing first started, knowing that an attempted escape would be too perilous, John and Li closed and barred the doors of the house. Gathering their families as well as Mei and the carrier together, they all bowed in prayer, imploring God to protect them.

The Stams' house and courtyard were surrounded by four windowless brick walls. Before long a group of Communist soldiers began to batter against the door at the back of the courtyard, breaking through it after a half-dozen violent blows. They next proceeded to the door of the house and started thundering against it to similarly break it down.

Inside the house John asked, "What shall we do? Shall we let them in or not?"

"If we don't let them in it's all over, and if we do it's the same," Li answered in despair.

"I'll open the door and welcome them," John decided. "We can entertain them."

"Whether we entertain them or not, it's all over," Li reiterated hopelessly.

Together John and Betty opened the door and greeted the soldiers. Four soldiers armed with rifles entered the house. They were dressed in gray uniforms, with straw sandals on their feet. Their caps had visors and a red star-shaped badge. One of them, an officer, wore a gray overcoat. They were all young men who looked to be in their early twenties.

Bowing, John said, "You have gone through much hardship. What are your names?"

Disarmed by this unexpected reception, the soldiers politely shared their names and in turn asked John his. "You are a foreigner, aren't you?" the officer queried.

"I am an American."

"Do you have any medicine?" asked the officer.

"We have a bottle of ointment," John answered. "Here, let me get it for you." Retrieving the bottle, he gave it to the officer.

Beginning to look around the room at the Stams' possessions, the lead soldier further inquired, "Have you any especially good things you can give us?"

"Certainly," came John's ready reply. "Whatever you like I'll give you." He then handed several choice items to them, including a clock, watch, camera, and flashlight.

As he did so, Betty stepped forward and said politely, "All of you must be thirsty. Allow me to get you some tea and cake." She excused herself into the kitchen and, a few minutes later, returned with a cup of steaming tea and a piece of cake for each of the soldiers.

"Do you have any money?" the officer plied.

"I've just come here to Tsingteh. I haven't much money. We are serving God. My money comes from Shanghai a

13

month at a time, so I only have forty or fifty dollars. But you're welcome to take it and divide it among yourselves."

Taking the currency, the officer asked, "Do you have any more?"

"No, I don't," John responded truthfully.

The officer's face suddenly hardened. Turning to one of the other soldiers, he commanded, "Search him!" The rough frisking that followed produced no further money.

"Now you can come with me to the yamen to talk to my leader," said the officer. "You needn't be afraid," he added with a tinge of sarcasm in his voice. "You'll have a nice time, and then you can come back to your home again."

John and Betty were able to stand together and pray in front of the small gathering before he was led away by the quadrant of soldiers. "Mr. Li, look after Mrs. Stam," John instructed as he left.

Other soldiers entered the house. They tied together in bundles any items they thought would be of use to their cause and carried them off to their commanders. Communist soldiers were searched by their superiors each night to make sure that they were not withholding valuable goods for themselves.

Betty had gone into her bedroom with Helen. The soldiers asked Li and Mei, "Where is the foreign woman?"

Li responded courageously, "We're all born of one father and mother. Have a little virtue. This is a woman and she has just given birth to a baby three months ago. You've taken her husband, so why take her?"

The soldiers pointed their rifles at the cook and maid and snarled, "Who are you to tell us what to do? And how does this concern you? You're Chinese, they're foreigners."

The soldiers then called Betty out of her room. She

came to the door with Helen in her arms. Sitting down on the steps that led to the room, she said, "You've taken my husband. Why do you want me?"

"If you have money we don't take you. Otherwise you must come with us."

Handing the baby to Mei, Betty retrieved some bills from inside her clothing and gave them to the soldiers. "We want American bank notes," they demanded.

"I don't have any," Betty asserted.

"Yes, you do. Now hand them over."

"Mrs. Stam speaks the truth," Li intervened. "American notes are of no use in an inland city like this one. So the Stams use only our native currency."

"Then you will now come with us," the soldiers responded.

"But you just promised not to take me if I gave you money."

"Never mind that!" the soldiers snapped. Raising their guns at Betty, they commanded, "Now walk!"

At the risk of further raising the soldiers' ire, Li requested, "Please don't separate Mrs. Stam from her husband."

Mei, overwrought with grief, pleaded to be allowed to go with her mistress. She was deterred only when the impatient soldiers leveled their rifles at her and threatened, "If you try to follow us, we will shoot you down."

"It's all right," Betty whispered to her. "I know that you would come with me if you could. It's really better that you stay here. That way, if any trouble comes to us, you can look after the baby." Then, taking Helen with her, she left with the soldiers.

At the end of the afternoon, John was permitted to return to their home, once again being guarded by a group of four soldiers. Asking Mei to collect a bundle of diapers for the baby, he went into the storeroom to get some milk. The maid, on the verge of tears, divulged, "The stores have all been taken by the soldiers."

"It doesn't matter," the missionary replied. "God is high above all in heaven. Our Father knows. These little things are immaterial. Don't be afraid, Mrs. Mei. You sleep with old Mrs. Li tonight."

John and Betty, along with baby Helen, were held as prisoners at the magistrate's yamen. That evening, John penned a letter to China Inland Mission officials in Shanghai to inform them that they had been captured and were being held for ransom.

*Tsingteh, Anhwei*
*December 6, 1934*

*China Inland Mission,*
*Shanghai*

*Dear Brethren,*
*My wife, baby, and myself are today in the hands of the Communists, in the city of Tsingteh. Their demand is twenty thousand dollars for our release.*

*All our possessions and stores are in their hands, but we praise God for peace in our hearts and a meal tonight. God grant you wisdom in what you do, and us fortitude, courage, and peace of heart. He is able— and a wonderful Friend in such a time.*

*Things happened so quickly this A.M. They were in the city just a few hours after the*

*ever-persistent rumors really became alarming,
so that we could not prepare to leave in time.
We were just too late.*

*The Lord bless and guide you, and as for us,
may God be glorified whether by life or by death.*

*In Him,
John C. Stam*[2]

# two

John Stam's spirit of complete consecration to the work of Christ, regardless of the personal cost involved, was forged through the upbringing he received from his dedicated Christian parents. Their deep personal piety and untiring efforts in bringing others to a saving knowledge of Jesus Christ had an enormous impact on all of their children, leading each of them into active Christian service.

Surprisingly, Peter Stam, John's father, had been reared in an environment that was far from Christian. He grew up in the village of 't Zand in the province of North Holland, The Netherlands. There for three generations his family had operated the village tavern, a place where drinking, gambling, and other worldly activities took place.

Quick-witted and lively, Peter often entertained the young people of the town at the tavern. He discovered, however, that such a godless environment and lifestyle provided him with no lasting joy or peace. He suffered many restless nights because he feared death and eternity.

In the spring of 1890, Peter, then a young man, sailed from Holland to the United States where he hoped to make his fortune. The voyage was a stormy one, and through it he was impressed with the power of God as seen in both the forces of nature and the preserving of life. This had a sobering effect on the young immigrant, turning him away, early on, from a life of wickedness.

Shortly after his arrival in America he met a zealous Christian woman named Margaret Neighmond. After learning that he was from Holland, she gave him a New Testament printed in both Dutch and English. "Here, Peter," she encouraged him, "take and study this Bible. It will help you to learn English."

"Oh, thank you, ma'am!" he responded sincerely. He was eager to learn to read and speak English to assist him in getting along in America.

"Lord God," the woman murmured as they parted company that day, "please help Peter to learn more than English through the reading of Your Word. Help him come to know the Savior, too."

Peter immediately began an intensive study of English from the book. As he read in the weeks that followed, his interest did switch more to spiritual concerns as he was confronted with the Bible's teaching that he was lost in sin. At first his proud nature strongly objected, but gradually he had to admit that it was true.

Eventually he read and reflected on John 3:16: "It says that 'God so loved the *world*,' and that surely includes me. It also says that 'He gave His only begotten Son, that *whosoever* believeth in Him should not perish,

19

but have everlasting life.' That, too, means me."

Then and there his heart was opened, and he bowed in prayer: "O God, I believe Your Word and I receive Christ as my Savior. Please forgive my sin and give me Your gift of eternal life. I surrender my life to Him Who died for me. From now on I will seek to serve You and others with my life."

In time Peter moved to Paterson, New Jersey, where he met a committed young Christian woman named Amelia Williams. She, along with her family, had immigrated to America from Holland. A friendship developed between them, and they were wed in January of 1892.

Not long into their married life the couple faced a test of their shared faith. One Saturday evening, shortly after their first child had been born, Peter was building a cradle. Totally unexpectedly he received a visit from his employer, a carpenter with whom he had worked for some time.

The man, who was not the easiest to work for, announced, "I need you to come to work tomorrow morning. I've got a rush job to get finished up."

The young husband and father paused thoughtfully. The additional income would be very helpful. He certainly needed a job right now and did not want to risk his by offending his employer. Still, he knew the clear teaching of Scripture about reserving the Sabbath for worship and rest. He swallowed hard, and then said calmly but firmly, "I'm sorry, but I cannot work tomorrow. You see, I'm a Christian, and I must observe the Lord's Day."

The employer reddened in anger and retorted brusquely, "Then you are out of work!"

After the man left, Amelia sought to reassure her husband: "You did the right thing, dear. We'll just have to accept this disappointment with the faith that the Lord will provide something else for us."

They did not have long to wait. Before they retired to bed that same evening a second knock came at the door. The caller was a messenger from another of Peter's former employers.

"The boss would like you to come back to work for him," the man informed Peter. "He's even willing to pay you a higher wage than you received before. He'd like you to begin first thing Monday morning."

That experience was never forgotten, and Peter repeatedly related it to his children as they were growing up. "Just let that remind you and encourage you," he would say to them, "to serve the Lord, not counting the cost. He'll always provide for you."

A short while after that initial test of obedience and faith, God further blessed the Stams. Peter's father came from Holland to visit him and his new family. Before the father returned home he gave his son some money, money that could be used to buy land upon which he could build houses.

Peter was able to borrow money at interest to purchase necessary building supplies, and his career as a contractor and builder was launched. The high quality of his workmanship, as well as his integrity, became well known, and he was hired to construct many new homes in Paterson's growing suburbs. His business gradually expanded to include the selling of real estate and insurance, as well as the operation of a lumberyard.

The commitment that Peter made at the time of his conversion to serve Christ and others was not an empty one. Even as his business endeavors were getting off the ground, he began an active personal outreach ministry. At first he sought to evangelize Jews by distributing Christian literature to them and sharing his testimony. He also started a mission work to reach the underprivileged of Paterson. As the work grew, he recruited volunteer workers from various churches in town. Mission workers, led by Peter, ministered to the needs of people in jails and hospitals as well as in charity homes for the poor and elderly. Peter even ventured into factories and taverns or out along the streets to share the saving message of Jesus Christ with those who needed to hear it.

In addition, a neatly furnished mission hall was opened. Three times a week it was filled with people from the street, and the Gospel was proclaimed. That was just the beginning of the vibrant mission work that would play such an important role in the spiritual development of all of the Stam children, as well as hundreds of other people.

Peter Stam, led by the Spirit of God, had indeed planted the seeds of a godly heritage.

# three

Peter and Amelia Stam eventually had nine children, six sons and three daughters, one of whom died in infancy. On an elevated portion of Paterson called Temple Hill, Peter built a simple frame house for his growing family. The home was reached by climbing a steep flight of stairs from the street below. A unique feature of the home was an observation dome that was built above the attic. From there one could look out over the city and the Hudson River valley and even espy the distant skyline of New York.

Peter and Amelia sought to teach their children the Word of God with all diligence. When the table was set for meals three times every day, a Bible was always placed beside each person's plate. After all the family members gathered, they opened their Bibles and a chapter of Scripture was read around the table, with each person taking three or four verses. No food was ever served until prayer was offered and a chapter of Scripture had been read.

Peter and Amelia had conservative convictions and maintained strict discipline of their children. Such practices as smoking, dancing, and going to the theater were absolutely forbidden, not only for the sake of maintaining a blameless Christian testimony, but also to safeguard the children from spiritually harmful influences.

The Stams even chose not to have a radio in their home. Peter explained the rationale for that decision to his children by stating, "Your mother and I have seen too much of other children drinking in what, to them, is poison! Your souls are worth more to us than the whole world."

These earnest Christian parents sought to model before their children high moral standards. "We sought grace to live consistently," Peter later testified of their parenting efforts. "You are so often in your own way when you undertake to rear children!"

At that time Peter was a leading elder and a devoted Sunday school teacher at Paterson's Third Christian Reformed Church. He and his wife faithfully took their children to both Sunday school and church. In addition, the children attended catechism classes at the church on Saturdays.

Not far from their home on Temple Hill was The Christian Grammar School where all the Stam children were enrolled. Its excellent curriculum, which included regular instruction on the Bible and Christian doctrine, supplemented the spiritual training the children received at home and church. The children were thus steeped in the teachings of Scripture literally seven days a week.

The Stams fostered a love for good books and music

in their children from an early age. Many attractive books were supplied for the children's reading profit and pleasure. In addition, all the children were required to take music lessons. Peter was willing to go to considerable expense so that his children could gain quality musical training.

Gospel songbooks were as plentiful as Bibles in the Stam household. The family enjoyed numerous evenings spent singing together in the home, accompanied by one person on the piano and another on the organ. In time other instruments were added as well until the Stams had formed a small family orchestra. Family members had many opportunities to use their musical abilities in various facets of the Lord's work in which they were involved.

A generous ministry of hospitality also had a formative spiritual impact on the children as they were growing up. Hundreds of people were provided a meal or a place to sleep in the Stams' house. Sometimes their guests were spiritually or materially needy individuals from the community. At other times visiting missionaries and pastors stayed with the devoted family. To testify to their generous spirit, the Stams had a small bedroom set aside especially for visiting Christian workers.

Peter and Amelia had an intense interest in all types of both foreign and home mission work. Regularly, whether with their guests or just with their own children, the topic of conversation in the Stam household centered around some aspect of Christ's kingdom work, either at home or abroad.

Occasional family outings helped add further flavor to the children's upbringing. A day spent at the seashore or a trip to New York City provided a pleasant change of pace from the normal routine and responsibilities of life.

As the Stams' outreach ministry to the underprivileged of Paterson continued to grow, the need for a larger mission facility became apparent. In an excellent location in the heart of town Peter discovered a large livery stable that was no longer in use. Although the deserted building was full of cobwebs and rats, Peter at once saw the possibilities.

With contributions from an ever-growing number of Christian supporters, the building was bought for the then enormous sum of twelve thousand dollars, and an additional eight thousand dollars was spent renovating it. The stable was transformed into the Star of Hope Mission, complete with an auditorium large enough to seat six hundred people. In addition, the mission had rooms for an office, Sunday school and sewing classes, as well as twelve bedrooms for staff workers and transients.

Regular evangelistic meetings were held in the mission's auditorium. Zealous workers from the mission also went out to spread the Gospel in open-air meetings, cottage gatherings, door-to-door visitations, hospitals, prisons, and even asylums.

In the decades that followed, hundreds of people representing many different nationalities were led to faith in Christ through the mission's ministry. The Gospel message was eventually sent forth from the mission in more than forty languages. Scores of young people who received early Christian service experience at the mission went on to dedicate their lives to vocational ministry in the United States and many foreign countries.

As the Stams witnessed and participated in the growth of this phenomenal ministry, they adopted the statement of Samuel the prophet as their family motto: "Ebenezer. . . Hitherto hath the LORD helped us" (1 Samuel 7:12, KJV).

"Actually," Peter loved to say, "to us it means 'hitherto hath the Lord done it all!' "

John Cornelius Stam, born on January 18, 1907, was Peter and Amelia's seventh child and fifth son. At less than a month old, he was dedicated to the Lord when he was baptized as an infant. His parents later testified, "We offered him, as we did all our other children, for the Lord's service as the Lord saw fit."

John was slower in embracing the Christian faith than were his siblings, which was due in part to his independent nature. Though eager to be helpful, John preferred to do things on his own. Even as a very young boy he would sew a button back on a piece of clothing rather than ask his mother to do it. Once when a tree needed to be uprooted, (after John was older), he readily did the job himself instead of waiting for others to help him.

After John's graduation from The Christian Grammar School, Peter offered to assist him financially in pursuing a higher education. But John was interested in going into business. He attended the Drake Business School for two years where he took up bookkeeping and stenography. Though only fifteen years old when he enrolled, he was already over six feet tall and possessed a manly appearance that made him look more like twenty.

On the outside John may have seemed determined and confident, but on the inside he felt restless and even upset. What he wanted out of life was to succeed in business and gain a good degree of wealth by doing so. He knew that the training he was receiving would better prepare him to achieve his goals. Still, he was not happy or at peace. Something was out of place in his life.

John was accustomed to seeing drunkards and other morally destitute people be converted and remarkably transformed at the mission. "But I'm not like them," he thought to himself. "I've gone to church and been a Christian all my life. I live a good moral life."

During the spring of 1922, however, he became deeply convicted of his own sinfulness. Things came to a head late that May when a blind itinerant evangelist named Thomas Houston came to conduct a series of special meetings at the Star of Hope Mission. As Houston gave an invitation at the end of his Sunday evening message he used a tactic employed by some evangelists of that era to encourage people to make a commitment to Christ. "If you are here tonight without Christ," he said, "I want you to stand up right where you're at. Go ahead, now, don't be bashful. It's important that you be honest with yourself about how you really stand before the Lord tonight."

The evangelist paused briefly as a handful of individuals who were under conviction humbly rose to their feet. A moment later Houston continued, "You may be seated. Now, if you are here tonight with Jesus as your personal Savior, I want you to stand."

John was seated near the back of the auditorium beside his brothers Jake and Neil. He knew that he could not rightly stand, but he was too embarrassed to remain seated, so he stood anyway. Jake, who was aware of the spiritual struggle his brother had been going through, wrongly concluded that John's standing meant that he had surrendered his life to Christ. Turning to John he said, "Praise the Lord! You're a Christian. Why don't you go up front to make your commitment public?"

John declined, knowing what was really going on in his heart. A few minutes later, he and Neil left the meeting before it was concluded and made their way home.

After the rest of the family arrived home that evening, Neil confided to Jake, "Both John and I were convicted of our sin and accepted Jesus as our Savior tonight. We didn't have enough courage to confess Christ in the open meeting, so we slipped out early. But we gave our lives to Him tonight."

Jake was overjoyed and had prayer with his two younger brothers. Afterward he wrote in the margin of his study Bible beside Acts 16:31: " 'And thy house'— May 28, 1922, Cornelius Stam and John Stam decided for Christ, believing on Him." The joyous news was quickly shared with the rest of the family that night.

The next day, however, John went to school more heavyhearted than ever. "I, too, am a sinner," he had to admit to himself. "Only rather than drunkenness or debauchery, my primary sin has been self-righteousness. I thought all my Bible reading and church attendance and service activities made me good enough for God. How deceived and prideful I've been!

"I've never actually accepted Jesus as my personal Savior. If I were to die right now, I'd step into eternity without Him. When I stood before God to be judged, He would not see me as righteous, but as having rejected His Son as my source of salvation. The result of my Christless life here on earth would be all eternity spent apart from God in hell.

"And to make matters worse, I've lied and misled my family about my being a Christian. I'm a hypocrite."

John did not delay further to do what he knew he needed to in order to correct the spiritual problems in his life. That same morning, while sitting at his desk in the classroom, he privately prayed to receive Christ as his Savior and Lord.

Teenage self-consciousness kept John from taking a public stand for Christ immediately after his conversion. He dreaded the prospect of being called on to speak in a street meeting, fearing that his school friends might see and laugh at him. If he happened upon a group from the mission that was singing or preaching in the open air, he went far out of his way so he wouldn't be spotted.

Still, inwardly he was desirous that the Lord's work would go forward in town. Summer was normally a time of active outdoor evangelism, with a team going out from the mission to share the Gospel in streets and parks. As that summer began, however, John saw that no such open-air endeavors were underway.

Concerned, he inquired of his father, "Why isn't the band out preaching?"

"It's up to you, John, to make a beginning," came the reply.

"Me?!" John exclaimed, stunned by the unexpected response. "Why me?"

"Because we don't have anyone else to lead that ministry this summer. You're old enough now to do that, John. I think you should consider it."

With considerable trepidation and rather halfheartedly at first, John took up his father's challenge. Soon his fears vanished and his heart was filled with joy and blessing. Many evenings that summer he and his younger brother, Neil, ventured out to witness for Christ on various street corners.

John completed his training at the business college the following year. Then over the course of the next six years he held office positions in Paterson and New York City. But it was no longer his ambition in life to gain great wealth through business. Instead, his interests and desires increasingly came to reflect eternal spiritual values.

His work in New York further expanded his view of the world. The office where he was employed over-looked the city's shipping yards. There he witnessed people and freight arriving from and going out to coun-tries all around the globe. Sometimes he walked down the city's famous shopping boulevards, Broadway and Fifth Avenue, observing the dazzling displays of opu-lence. On other occasions he ventured into Chinatown or other ethnic neighborhoods where he witnessed squalor and deprivation.

Wherever he went John saw thousands of people who needed the Lord. Gradually an unshakable convic-tion developed in his heart: He needed to leave his secu-lar career and devote himself to full-time evangelistic ministry. When, in 1929 at age 22, he announced his res-ignation, his employer, not wanting to lose a capable and reliable employee, protested and forcefully sought to dissuade him. But John's mind was made up.

For the next several months he served full-time in the ministry of the Star of Hope Mission. During that time Peter and Amelia Stam made a trip to their homeland of Holland, leaving the mission under the supervision of John and Neil while they were away. Some interpersonal conflicts surfaced among the mission workers and atten-dance at meetings started to dwindle.

John became discouraged with the situation and him-self. One morning as he was praying about the matter, he stated, "I am the wrong man to have anything to do with overseeing this mission work."

Just then he lifted his eyes and caught sight of a plaque hanging on the opposite wall that contained a

Scripture text. The plaque had been there for months, but John had never before taken note of its message. The text was Psalm 18:32 (KJV): "It is God that girdeth me with strength, and maketh my way perfect."

Heartened by the verse, John was able to carry on faithfully in the ministry entrusted to him. Nevertheless, that challenging experience helped him to realize that he needed further training in order to be more adequately prepared for the demands of vocational ministry.

In the weeks that followed he prayerfully concluded that the Lord would have him enroll in the practical Bible training course at the Moody Bible Institute in Chicago.

# *four*

B etty Stam, like her husband John, was raised in an environment of consecrated Christian service. Her father, Charles Ernest Scott, was reared in a staunch Presbyterian home in Alma, Michigan. The son of a Civil War officer, Charles early on developed a deep and abiding interest not only in the Bible but in American history as well.

After graduating from Alma College, he went on to earn a Master of Arts degree in history from the University of Pennsylvania in 1899. He next was a Fellow at the University of Munich in Germany for a year. There he met the young woman he would later marry, Clara Emily Heywood, who was also studying at the university.

Returning to the States, Charles attended Princeton Theological Seminary where he studied under the esteemed evangelical theologian Benjamin B. Warfield. After graduating from Princeton in 1903 with a doctor of philosophy degree, Charles then married Clara that September.

With his impressive academic credentials, Charles had attractive vocational opportunities in prominent church and college settings. These he declined, however, sensing that the Lord was calling him instead to devote his life to missionary service. He first served as a Presbyterian home missionary in the woods of northern Michigan. After that he pastored the First Church of Albion, Michigan, for two years.

Charles and Clara's first child, Elisabeth Alden Scott, was born on February 22, 1906, in Albion. Her middle name was chosen in honor of the early American settlers John and Priscilla Alden, who arrived on the *Mayflower*. Clara, originally from Holyoke, Massachusetts, was a descendant of the Aldens.

Six months after Betty's birth the Scotts sailed to China, settling in the northern province of Shantung. Serving under the auspices of the Presbyterian Board, U.S.A., they carried out a dual ministry of evangelism and Bible teaching.

Charles and Clara first lived in the coastal city of Tsingtao. There they had four more children, two daughters, Beatrice and Helen, and two sons, Francis and Kenneth. The setting was an idyllic one for the Scott children. They spent a great deal of time outdoors, exploring the wooded countryside, playing at the seashore, and trying to ride their father's antiquated bicycle. Even their schooling was carried out in an open-air setting by a cousin who came to live with them as their teacher.

Dr. and Mrs. Scott, though heavily involved in various ministry activities, invested much personal time and attention in the upbringing of their children. Their family motto was "do it together," and that is precisely how they approached life.

Immediately after breakfast they had family prayers, a time when each of the children took turns praying and choosing the songs to be sung. At eleven every morning Charles would break away from his ministry responsibilities to join his children outdoors for an hour of vigorous running games until noon dinner was served. After lunch all the children were required to lie down for a time of rest. Finally, following an early supper, they shared a family reading hour in which Charles or Clara read from beautifully illustrated children's books.

The Scotts normally did not take their children to the long Chinese church services in Tsingtao. Instead, they worshiped with them and instructed them from the Bible in their own home. Helen would later write: "I think that our father and mother must have taken their career as parents more seriously than most people; for as we look back upon it all—the careful training, the many activities they shared with us, and the mental attitudes they so carefully instilled—we marvel at the work they must have put into it."[1]

The Scott children had friendly but somewhat restricted relations with the Chinese. Their servants were all devoted Christians, and the children had genuine love and affection for them, especially the old amah who cared for and "bossed" them. The children used to sneak out to the servants' rooms to eat Chinese food, even though their mother thought such a diet was not good for them.

As a young adult, Betty wrote a poem for her parents entitled "To Father and Mother" in which she expressed her deep love and appreciation for them and for her upbringing:

My words, dear Father, precious Mother,
    May God select them from His rich store.
I am, because you loved each other—
    Oh, may my love unite you more!

When I was born, brimmed the bright water,
    For pain and joy, in eyes gray-blue.
(A tiny bud of you, a daughter;
    And yet, distinct, a person too!)

In pain and joy and love upwelling,
    You treasured me against your heart;
And I, bewildered beyond telling,
    Grew calm and slept, with tears astart.

As life grew bigger, I stood firmer,
    With legs apart, eyes round and wide.
You told me all I asked, a learner
    Who was not ever satisfied!

Throughout my childhood flitted fairies
    Of sunshine and the open air,
Came chubby sisters, cheeked with cherries,
    And baby boys with kewpie-hair.

We grew like colts and April saplings—
    Seeking rebelliously for Truth.
You loved and learned and stood beside us,
    And understood the shocks of youth.

As life grew mystical and magic
    And I walked dreamily on earth,
Ere I should wake to see the tragic,

You planted, deep, ideals of worth.

You fed my mind, a flamelet tiny,
    Yet keen and hungry, in a wood;
It seized and glowed and spread and crackled,
    And all the fuel in reach was good.

Somewhere beneath the loam of senses,
    A seed of Art you hoped was there,
Received the sun and rain and blossomed,
    All through your stimulating care.

But not content with mental culture,
    Seeing my spirit mourn in night,
You taught the Word and Way for sinners,
    Until Christ's Spirit brought me light.

Your loving courage never faltered,
    Your plans were gently laid aside,
(That time my whole life-pattern altered)
    Obedient to our Lord and Guide.

Your life for others, in each other,
    Shines through the world, pain-tarnished here;
As faithful stewards, Father, Mother,
    Your crown shall be unstained by tear.

Imagine, in God's certain Heaven,
    Your children made forever glad,
Praising the Lord for having given
    The dearest parents ever had.[2]

Eventually those exceptionally happy years in

Tsingtao came to an end. As a young teen Betty was sent to a coeducational boarding school in Tungchow not far from Peking to further her education. A short while after that the rest of the Scott family relocated to Tsinan. In time Betty's sisters and brothers followed her to the school in Tungchow.

The Scott children were able to spend Christmas and summer vacations at their parents' home in Tsinan. The oppressively hot summer months were spent at the family's cottage at Peitaiho, another seaside resort. There the children spent most of their time swimming, playing tennis, and reading. They were also able to carry out various secretarial responsibilities to assist their father with his ever-pressing ministry demands.

When Betty was seventeen her parents were due to take a furlough in the United States. The Scotts knew that Betty would remain in the States to attend college and that this was likely the final year they would spend together as a family. Desiring to give their children the opportunity to see more of the world, they invested six full months in traveling about several countries in the Middle East and Europe en route to America. During that time, the Scotts visited Egypt, the Holy Land, Greece, Italy, Switzerland, France, and England.

Scores of memorable experiences were packed into those exciting months. Their spirits were deeply stirred in Palestine as they visited Calvary where Jesus was crucified and the garden tomb from which He was resurrected. In Egypt they rode on donkeys across the scorching plains to visit the gigantic pyramids that housed the tombs of the ancient pharaohs. In Switzerland, by contrast, they walked on glaciers and climbed Mount Jungfrau, eating chocolate and singing heartily as they trekked along mountain roads.

They explored cathedrals and art galleries in Europe, and happened to be at St. Peter's in Rome on a day when the Pope was there to canonize a new saint.

Some of Betty's memories from those travels, along with her bright outlook on life, were put to words in her poem "Traveler's Song":

I sought for beauty on the earth,
    And found it everywhere I turned;
A precious stone from Singapore
    That sapphire shone and sapphire burned—
A Rajah's ransom it was worth.

Eternal grandeur brooded deep
    In Egypt's pyramids of stone,
And still I smell the orange bloom;
    I see the frosty stars that shone
And cooled the tranquil Nile to sleep.

I loved the skies of Italy,
    The swarthy, singing boatmen there,
The Virgins of the Renaissance,
    With grave, sweet eyes and golden hair—
The land of Art and Melody.

Lingers long into the night
    On snowy peaks the Alpine glow,
And every lake is loveliest,
    And there, amid the endless snow,
I picked the edelweiss so white.

Before a Chinese city gate,
    The entrance to an ancient town,

I saw the men fly dragon-kites;
 While, by the willows weeping down,
Their wives beat clothes, from dawn till late.

Then home I came, as though on wings,
 The joy of life in heart and eyes;
For, everything was glorified—
 The earth, the ocean, and the skies,
And even all the common things![3]

Another indicator of Charles and Clara Scott's parenting success is seen in the favorable perspective that each of their children maintained toward the prospect of missionary work. Writing of their feelings as they left China on the traveling furlough, Helen said, "All five of us children expected at that time to return to China as missionaries. Our parents never urged it, but it seemed the natural and right thing to do."[4]

While at the boarding school in Tungchow, Betty and Helen had studied Chinese for two years, learning to read and write the language. At that time they supposed that they would need it in the future. As it turned out, each of the Scott children did serve as missionaries in China as adults.

A short while after the Scotts arrived back in America for the latter half of their furlough, Betty suffered a serious bout of rheumatic fever. The painful illness left her heart so weakened that for months afterward she had to lie flat on her back in bed.

Yet out of that difficult period came one priceless blessing: Betty discovered her gift for writing poetry.

# *five*

I n the fall of 1924, nearly a year after the Scotts
arrived in the United States on furlough, Betty's
health was sufficiently recovered to allow her to enter
Wilson College in Chambersburg, Pennsylvania. There
she gained the respect of her fellow students due to her
mature, spiritual outlook on life and her exceptional literary gifts.

Betty became the president of the college's literary
society and an associate editor of the society's publication. In addition, she served on the student government
cabinet, participated in some drama productions, and
was an active member of the school's Student Volunteer
Organization, which promoted interest in foreign missions. Despite her extracurricular activities and commit-
ments, Betty excelled academically, graduating magna
cum laude in 1928 with a bachelor of arts degree.

During the summer between her first two years of

college, Betty attended a Christian conference in Keswick, New Jersey, that had a profound impact on her spiritual life. There she fully consecrated herself to the Lord, and afterward she wrote to her parents of her experience:

*"Keswick" is over, but I trust never the message! Thank the Lord! I have now surrendered myself to the Lord more than I have ever realized was possible. I have never realized that such victory was possible. The Way is just Christ—and complete consecration to His will in our lives. Among other things, I have dedicated to Him whatever I have of poetic or literary gift. Maybe He can use me along that line. Wouldn't it be wonderful!*

*Giving my life to Jesus makes me see what I ought to have done long ago, and I wonder how I can have been so dumb before. Now that sounds as though I were a perfect little angel, flapping my wings 'round! But, of course, I'm awfully imperfect still, or as one might put it, future-perfect—which means that there is promise for the future. Even now, when I put first the pleasure, interests, and point of view of others, everything goes along most gaily.*

*"Keswick" has been a wonderful revelation to me of how victorious the victorious life really is. Since being there I have had my prayers answered in most definite ways. Now the Lord is showing me how necessary it is to rise early in the morning to read His Word, and He is helping me to wake and get up in time to do so.*

*I don't know what God has in store for me. I*

*really am willing to be an old-maid missionary,*
*or an old-maid anything else, all my life, if God*
*wants me to. It's as clear as daylight to me that*
*the only worthwhile life is one of unconditional*
*surrender to God's will, and of living in His*
*way, trusting His love and guidance.* [1]

At Keswick Betty adopted Philippians 1:21 as her life verse: "For to me to live is Christ, and to die is gain." There, too, she started praying, "O God, if You so will, may nothing prevent me from returning someday to China as a missionary."

After graduating from Wilson, Betty entered the Moody Bible Institute in Chicago. She desired to gain practical experience in leading people to Christ, rather than theoretically discussing evangelism or theology, and she soon had her opportunity. As she began participating in prison ministry and street meetings, her reserved, sensitive spirit at first shrank at the prospect of taking an active role. But once she took the plunge, she discovered that the stretching outreach endeavors helped her develop greater spiritual poise and provided her with considerable joy.

Betty's friends and acquaintances at both Wilson and Moody have described her as quiet, gentle, gracious, and sincere. Though naturally reserved, she was friendly and interested in others. Fellow students often sought her out as a trustworthy confidante and counselor. Deep personal serenity and faith in God were also among her outstanding characteristics. She never seemed hurried or ruffled.

Her dress, while always appropriate, was never showy. She did not wear any jewelry. She parted her dark, straight hair on one side and gathered it in a knot at the back of her neck. Her rounded face had a soft, sweet appearance, and her eyeglasses gave her a studious look.

Betty's willingness to serve the Lord by spreading the Gospel was reflected in "A Song of Sending," a poem she wrote after her first year at Moody:

When Christ the Savior lived on earth,
    Long, long ago, long years ago,
He bade us tell to all the world,
    "God loves you so! He loves you so!"
He gave command to heal the sick
    From sin-wrought woe, all sin-wrought woe;
He said to cleanse the leper too,
    As white as snow, yes, white as snow.

Lord Jesus, Thou art waiting still.
    We hear Thee call, so clearly call;
"Who love Me, forth! and follow me.
    Though weak and small, so weak and small.
In God's own Spirit shall he go,
    He shall not fall, no never fall;
That man I need to move the world,
    Who gives Me all, to Me his all."

See, all the careless multitudes
    Are passing by, now passing by.
The world is sick with sin and woe.
    All men must die, some day must die.
The time set for our Lord's return
    Is drawing nigh, draws ever nigh.
Send us in all Thy cleansing power—
    Lord, here am I! Here, Lord, am I![2]

Betty spent much time in prayer about exactly where God would have her serve Him once her Bible institute training was completed. "Lord, You know that in my heart I long to return to China," she honestly confessed. "But I fear that my desire may be too heavily influenced by my love for my parents and the thought of being back home. I truly want to serve in the place where You would have me to be. Please make Your will clear to me."

For a time the needs in Africa, especially among lepers, were pressed upon her heart and mind. "There seem to be so few individuals who are willing to dedicate themselves to ministering to that needy group of people." She wrestled with her own thoughts. "Such a ministry seems so Christlike. Yet what a difficult task it would be! Am I willing to give up the dear prospects of China in order to serve God in that way?"

"Yes, Lord," she was eventually able to pray, "I will serve You by ministering to lepers in Africa if Your hand so leads."

God blessed her further step of surrender with a sense of reassurance that she wrote of in a poem entitled "My Testimony":

And shall I fear
    That there is anything that men hold dear
Thou would'st deprive me of,
    And nothing give in place?
That is not so—
    For I can see Thy face
And hear Thee now:

"My child, I died for thee.
    And if the gift of love and life

You took from Me,
   Shall I one precious thing withhold—
One beautiful and bright
   One pure and precious thing withhold?
My child, it cannot be."[3]

During her second year at Moody she sent the autobiographical poem "Stand Still and See" to her parents. "This poem," she explained, "expresses the distress of soul and fear of mind that were mine before I surrendered my all—even inmost motives, so far as I know—to God's control. The fourth stanza is His gracious acceptance of my unworthy self; the last tells the joy, satisfaction, and peace of assured guidance that Christ my Savior gives me, now that He is Lord of my life."[4]

I'm standing, Lord:
   There is a mist that blinds my sight.
Steep, jagged rocks, front, left and right,
   Lower, dim, gigantic, in the night.
Where is the way?

I'm standing, Lord:
   The black rock hems me in behind,
Above my head a moaning wind
   Chills and oppresses heart and mind.
I am afraid!

I'm standing, Lord:
   The rock is hard beneath my feet;
I nearly slipped, Lord, on the sleet.
   So weary, Lord! and where a seat?
Still must I stand?

He answered me, and on His face
    A look ineffable of grace,
Of perfect, understanding love,
    Which all my murmuring did remove.


I'm standing, Lord:
    Since Thou hast spoken, Lord, I see
Thou hast beset—these rocks are Thee!
    And since Thy love encloses me,
I stand and sing.[5]


In the end, God providentially and clearly opened the door for Betty to serve Him in China. He used this experience, however, to deepen her willingness to embrace His will for her life, whatever that might prove to be.

# six

John Stam arrived at Moody Bible Institute as Betty Scott was beginning her second year there, in the fall of 1929. He immediately found himself among a thousand students, most of whom shared his desire to grow in the knowledge of the Lord and in the ability to serve Him well.

John at first enrolled in the Missionary Course, which included training in a number of practical ministry subjects. A year later, sensing his need for a more thorough knowledge of the Scriptures, he transferred to the General Bible Course. He applied himself in his studies and was able to achieve high grades.

His teachers saw in him above average abilities, character, drive, and potential. The secretary of the faculty would later write of him: "He was a young man of arresting personality and unusual Christian character. He was well balanced and energetic, possessing good judgment and considerable initiative. In his Practical Christian Work he proved to be a good speaker and an exceptionally good group leader."

One school official stated of John, "He will undoubtedly be heard from." Another predicted, "Expect to see this young man make good in a large way."[1]

His fellow students also thought highly of him. They appreciated his intensely committed yet down-to-earth approach to the Christian life. One of his classmates later testified about him, "He had a passion for souls. His personal work was exemplary, in that he was always at it. But John was not ascetic in any way. One could have plenty of fun on a trip or at a picnic with him. He was a regular fellow, if ever there was one."[2]

Despite such praise, John was virtually unaware that others held him in high esteem. Indeed, he was well aware of his own shortcomings. "My only trouble is myself," he wrote candidly to one of his brothers.

John soon became involved in a number of the student prayer meetings that met each week. Because of his taxing schedule he found it difficult to squeeze in a daily personal quiet time with the Lord, and it was not long before his spiritual life and activity began to feel lifeless and mechanical. To maintain spiritual vibrancy he established the discipline of getting up at five each morning to spend a season alone with God in prayer and the study of His Word.

John entered Moody with a definite openness to the prospect of serving overseas someday should the Lord so direct him. He had been raised in a home where interest in and support for a variety of foreign missionary causes was always strong. One of his brothers was already serving in the Belgian Congo of Africa.

Some of the prayer meetings John participated in at Moody focused considerable attention on the needs of various missionary endeavors. As he read numerous prayer letters from around the globe, his heart was further stirred over the significant opportunities and crying needs for spreading the Gospel in largely unevangelized parts of the world.

One of these prayer groups was the Monday evening meeting sponsored by the China Inland Mission (CIM). That group met in the home of Mr. and Mrs. Isaac Page, themselves highly committed missionaries who at the time were serving as CIM representatives in the Midwest. It was through those meetings that John met Betty Scott.

John became perplexed that year when his parents, writing letters to him, did not seem to be supportive of his inclination to commit his life to foreign missionary service. Peter Stam was getting older and knew that a younger man would be needed in the not-too-distant future to assume the leadership of the Star of Hope Mission. For some time he had secretly cherished the hope that John would return to do so after completing his training at Moody.

"Every man's life is a plan of God," was Peter's deep conviction that he often shared with others, including his own children. "Young people should not be swayed by merely human influences or personal desires in their choice of a lifework. And they should not overlook the need at home." Peter wrote John to express a concern: "I fear that sometimes speakers and missionary societies try to persuade young people, through emotions, to choose the foreign work."

John was nonplused. He loved his parents and did not want to disappoint them. He was open to serving wherever God would have him. Yet somehow the needs overseas, where far fewer Christian workers were available, seemed more pressing than those at home.

He expressed his sentiments in a letter to his brother Jacob in Paterson: "The Lord knows where He wants me, whether in Holland, in Paterson, or some other place in the States, in China, or in India. However, it does look frightfully disproportionate to see so many here in comparison with the few over yonder. We know that the Lord's work is not overstaffed here, but, as someone has said, 'There are those who simply cannot go and those who are free to go. Why should both stay at home for the same work?' "[3]

John made this a matter of earnest prayer. Gradually he came to see a shift in the outlook expressed in his father's letters. "Why think of China or India," Peter wrote several weeks later, "when there are other countries more open? Would it not seem more in keeping with the Lord's will to go where work can be unhindered, rather than where life is always in danger and there is so much opposition?"

Eventually, after several more months had passed, the father wrote his son: "May the Lord richly bless you and guide you by His Holy Spirit to do His will. We must pray that more men may go to China."[4]

By June of 1930 John was becoming increasingly burdened about conditions in China. Communist rebels had seized control of much of Kiangsi Province in southeastern China, leading to widespread bloodshed and loss of life. Missionaries were not spared in the unrest. Three CIM associates had already been killed and two others were still being held captive.

Of this situation John wrote to a brother: "It is an amazing thing that the provinces in China which are having most trouble are the very provinces in which the China Inland Mission has, after prayerful consideration, decided to press forward evangelistic efforts. Two of their most valued workers, Mr. and Mrs. R. W. Porteous, are still in the hands of bandits, but reports have come through that they are teaching and preaching daily among their captors. It is said that the Communist soldiers like them so well that they declare that 'these old people are too good to kill.' They wish they would become Communists! With all its internal troubles, there seem to be unparalleled opportunities in China."[5]

As it turned out, the very next day after John penned those words, the Porteouses were released. Their captivity had lasted exactly one hundred days.

When John went to Moody, he had some money saved up to help pay for his first year's tuition as well as room and board. His family members assumed that when his personal funds were depleted he would let them know of his need so they could assist him financially. He determined, however, that he would not do that.

He knew that if God led him into mission work, whether at home or abroad, there would be many times when he would need to trust the Lord alone to supply his financial needs. His time at Moody would provide the perfect opportunity to develop the strong faith that would be needed for that type of service. Rather than looking to others for assistance, he would speak only to God about his needs, and would trust Him to supply them.

Believing it the responsible thing to do, John held a part-time job waiting on tables in the college cafeteria. His diligence, efficiency, and helpfulness were appreciated, and in time he became the supervisor of both the dining hall and the kitchen. While this work helped to meet some of his financial obligations, it could not possibly supply all of them. By the time the spring quarter arrived in his first year at Moody he began looking in faith to God to provide what he could not. That proved to be the case throughout the remainder of his time in school.

On Saturday, November 15, 1930, John made this entry in his personal journal: "Life has become exceedingly interesting lately. Since I have acted on the assumption that whether I work for the Lord at home or abroad I need to be ready to trust Him for my temporal needs, I have had some opportunity to prove that God is faithful. Now I am at the end of my rope. Next Tuesday I owe the Accounting Department ten dollars. If I do not pay it, I am in debt. The command is: 'Owe no man anything.' God's commands are His enablings, but He cannot answer our prayers if our lives are not cleansed. 'Search me, O God.' 'In Thee do I trust.' 'Put me not to shame.' Oh, for a closer walk with God."

The following Monday evening, John and another student took a long walk with Isaac Page. They conversed about the need to trust God for His financial provision while seeking to faithfully carry out His will. John said nothing about his present needs but, in confidence, shared some of the specific ways in which the Lord had cared for him as he had endeavored to live by faith during the previous summer.

Before they parted company that evening, Page pushed something into John's pocket. The surprised student discovered that it was a five-dollar bill.

The next morning, the day his bill was due, John went to check his mail. There he found a Moody Bible Institute envelope with his name written on it. The envelope contained $7.33. There was no letter with the money.

"Praise the Lord," John wrote in his diary that evening, "that bill has been paid on time. He is faithful. 'Bless the Lord, O my soul.' "[6]

The following month the scenario was repeated, with another school payment due that exceeded John's meager income. A friend and fellow student, LeRoy King, who had become aware of his challenging financial situation, approached him one evening. "I've been very much troubled thinking about your school bill, John. I believe the Lord would have me to help you pay it this month since I have the money on hand."

"Oh, Roy, I couldn't take your money," John quickly stated. "You're going to need that to cover your own expenses later on."

"I'll let God take care of that when the time comes," the friend responded. "For now I think He wants me to help you out."

The next day Roy dropped by to see John again, this time with the cash that was needed to complete the payment on his December school bill. When John hesitated further, Roy stated, "Look, John, you might as well take it and save me some trouble. Otherwise I'll just have to send it through the school mail box in care of your account."

John did accept the money. That night he recorded in his journal four lessons learned through that experience: "First, I expected and prayed for funds, rather dictating to the Lord the way in which they should come, or should not come, my last thought being Roy. The Lord, however, used the very ordinary rather than the miraculous. The Lord deliver me further from always looking for the miraculous, and hoping to have my faith strengthened in that way.

"Secondly, I promised the Lord that I would testify as to His faithfulness in supplying my needs in answer to prayer, and in keeping me out of debt. But I now see that if the Lord had answered so, it would have engendered spiritual pride, and such a testimony might seem to be a rebuke to those who are working their way through school, for not having more faith, and to those who are in debt, for not having faith.

"Thirdly, it has taught me what it means to be under obligation to others for my needs. Some more self-sufficiency shattered!

"Fourthly, what it means to be 'of no reputation.' All in all this day has been very fruitful."[7]

Another Moody student from Paterson offered John a ride home that holiday break. John knew that the trip would be a long, cold one, but he did not have even enough money to buy a heavy pair of socks to keep his feet warm in the car. Then one of the few shirts he had intended to take home with him ripped as he was putting it on one evening. He did not want to wear a mended shirt at home because then his parents would guess that his finances were low and would insist on providing his material needs.

Feeling somewhat downcast, he went for a walk along Lake Michigan. As he strolled along the beach he thought to himself, "Well, it's all right to trust the Lord, but I wouldn't mind having a few dollars in my pocket." Immediately he felt convicted in his own mind: "To think that I'm valuing a few dollars in my pocket above the Lord's ability to provide a million if I need it!"

A few minutes later, as he was crossing Michigan Avenue, he looked down and spotted a perfectly good, though wet, five-dollar bill lying on the busy street. "Oh, what a rebuke it was from the Lord!" he later said. "Just one of those gentle rebukes the Lord can so wonderfully give us."

Picking up the bill, he took it back to his dorm and dried it out. The next day he visited the bargain counter at a nearby department store and bought two new shirts and a good pair of warm socks.

Shortly after that he was escorting a female student to her home following an evening meeting. As they walked along, she confided to him: "My one regret is that I have had to work so hard trying to work my way through school that it has been a drain on my health. If I were to do it over again, I would endeavor to live more by faith as you are doing."

"Living by faith?" John queried.

"Yes. I've heard of your trusting God to supply your needs rather than thinking you have to do it all yourself."

John was chagrined. He had always tried to be careful not to share with others his private faith venture lest he seem prideful or judgmental toward those who worked more or borrowed money to cover the cost of their education. But here was a fellow student who seemed well aware of his *modus operandi*.

Suddenly he remembered the private discussion he had had with Isaac Page and another student a month earlier. Apparently the words of personal testimony he had shared in confidence out of a sincere desire to glorify God had been passed on to others. The young woman whom John was escorting that evening was a regular participant in the CIM prayer group that met on Monday evenings. He supposed that she, and likely others as well, had learned this about him at that prayer fellowship.

Later that night John penned a mixture of conflicting thoughts in his diary: "It almost frightens me to think of the whole 'China bunch' probably knowing it by now. I certainly don't like being held up as a model. But it seems as if the die is cast, and perhaps it is of the Lord, that I have now gone too far to retrace my steps. At least that is my fear; suppose I weaken, and turn back—the Lord will surely not be glorified. 'No man, having put his hand to the plough, and looking back, is fit for the kingdom of God' (Luke 9:62). The die is cast—I believe that the Lord is leading."[8]

# seven

At the beginning of the following year, in January of 1931, John accepted the invitation of a small country church in Elida, Ohio, to become its interim pastor. Twice a month he traveled the two hundred miles from Chicago to Elida, where he not only filled the pulpit but also carried out an active visitation ministry. The remuneration John received for this ministry barely covered his expenses to carry it out. Nevertheless, he zealously and faithfully continued on until his graduation from Moody sixteen months later.

The student pastor encouraged his church people by exhortation and by example to commit Scripture to memory. He helped them to gain a fresh sense of the relevance of God's Word to their own lives. "Who has a verse of Scripture to share with us this morning?" he would ask each Sunday before the sermon. "Let me start us off. I've been thinking again this past week of Isaiah

26:3: 'Thou wilt keep him in perfect peace, whose mind is stayed on thee: because he trusteth in thee.'

"Now isn't that so true?" he might add. "If we'll only stay focused on God and His ability to help us handle any challenge or difficulty that comes into our lives, we will experience complete peace. We just need to trust Him. All right, who will be next to share?"

Frequently, up to fifteen minutes were devoted to various members of the congregation sharing Scripture verses. Among John's favorite verses were these two: "So that we may boldly say, The Lord is my helper, and I will not fear what man shall do unto me" (Hebrews 13:6, KJV); "But my God shall supply all your need according to his riches in glory by Christ Jesus" (Philippians 4:19, KJV). He also loved to dwell on the theme of faithfulness, both God's faithfulness to His children and the believer's need for faithfulness in the Christian life.

With his attractive tenor singing voice, John enthusiastically led the Elida congregation in singing "Great Is Thy Faithfulness" and numerous other hymns of praise. Periodically he brought other students from Moody to join him in singing and sharing at special meetings. On a couple of occasions they formed a quartet that the Elida folk dubbed "The Happy Four."

The church families took turns hosting John in their homes when he was with them for the weekend. They appreciated his personable, friendly manner with both adults and children.

"John was more than our minister," one congregant later shared. "He not only taught and preached but was our close and intimate friend also. He visited most if not all of us in our homes. He was quick to see a joke, and could be jolly and enjoy himself wherever he happened to be, especially where there were young folks and children. And they loved him greatly."[1]

John also paid visits to those in the community who did not attend a church. He ministered to Protestants, Catholics, and known unbelievers, adults and children, whoever was receptive to his friendly spiritual concern. These visits were often carried out on foot, leading him to undertake long walks in that rural community.

But the student pastorate was not without its pressures and discouragements. The long hours of travel and extra study time often taxed John's strength. At times his diligent efforts seemed to produce little fruit. But he optimistically, faithfully carried on without complaining. He viewed the ministry in Elida as a test to see whether he would likely ever be able to do anything for the Lord in China.

Another matter very much on John's heart during his second year at Moody was his deepening relationship with Betty Scott. He had first met her some eighteen months earlier at the CIM prayer group that gathered weekly in Isaac Page's home. John was quickly impressed by Betty's spiritual maturity and her fervency for missionary work. He appreciated her quiet, sincere spirit. It was not long before he began to take more note of the sweet face that complemented so well her friendly personality.

Betty, for her part, gained a favorable impression of John early on in their relationship as well. At six feet, two inches in height, he stood out in a crowd. He had handsome features, and his slightly receding hairline and rounded eyeglasses gave him a mature appearance.

Even more attractive to Betty was John's strong Christian character. His heart for the Lord and his burning desire to serve Him were obvious. He was friendly and courteous in his dealings with others. Inclined toward being a leader, he approached life with confidence and intensity, but he was not cocky or pushy. While he was full of zest for life and knew how to have fun, his overall outlook was a serious one.

John and Betty's relationship started out as a simple friendship but gradually began to deepen into mutual romantic attraction. They were very guarded in that respect, however. Paramount in both their minds was the determination to devote their lives to serving God wherever He might lead them. Should God direct them to different fields of service, they would not be able to cultivate a romantic relationship.

Several years earlier, at the age of eighteen, Betty had written a poem entitled "My Ideal" in which she had described the characteristics she would look for in a potential spouse:

I'll recognize my true love
    When first his face I see;
For he will strong, and healthy,
    And broad of shoulder be:
His movements will be agile,
    Quick, and full of grace;
The eyes of Galahad will smile
    Out of his friendly face.

His features won't be Grecian,
    Nor yet will they be rough;
His fingers will be flexible,
    Long, and strong, and tough:
Oh, he'll be tall, and active
    As an Indian,

With rounded muscles rippling out
    Beneath his healthy tan.

His interest is boundless
    In every fellow man;
He'll gladly be a champion
    As often as he can:
Oh, he'll be democratic,
    And maybe shock the prude;
He will not fawn before the great,
    Nor to the low be rude.

He'll be a splendid "mixer,"
    For he has sympathy;
Perhaps his most pronounced trait
    Is versatility;
If Providence should drop him
    In any foreign town,
He'd somehow speak the language
    And find his way around.

He'll have a sense of humor
    As kindly as it's keen;
He'll be a mighty tower
    On which the weak may lean.
His patience and unselfishness
    May readily be seen;
He's very fond of children,
    And children worship him.

He will not be a rich man,
    He has no earthly hoard;
His money, time, heart, mind and soul

Are given to the Lord.
He'll be a modern Daniel,
    A Joshua, a Paul;
He will not hesitate to give
    To God his earthly all.

He'll be, he'll be, my hero—
    A strong-armed fighting man,
Defender of the Gospel,
    And Christian gentleman.
Oh, if he asks a Question,
    My answer "Yes" will be!
For I would trust and cherish
    Him to eternity.[2]

John Stam seemed to fit her description remarkably well. Betty could not help but wonder if he might indeed be the one God intended for her. For the time being, though, there was no way of knowing for sure, and she would just have to leave the matter in the Lord's hands.

Increasingly, both John and Betty were sensing, independently of each other, that God was leading them toward service in China, very possibly with the CIM. They were both seeking the Lord's direction regarding their potential role in an expansion emphasis that the CIM was prayerfully promoting at that time.

Tumultuous political conditions in China throughout the 1920s had made missionary endeavors there anything but a safe, stable enterprise. More than a dozen different "governments," centered in various major cities, had arisen, and as the Communists, led by Mao Tse-tung, grew in power, several missionaries were killed at their instigation.

By 1927, as the armies of opposition leader Chiang

Kai-shek swept across southern China, thousands were left dead. In that year alone a staggering 50 percent of all foreign missionaries in China left, never to return. The majority of CIM missionaries were forced to leave their stations for a period of time to go to safer locations.

Two years later, however, Dixon Hoste, general director of the CIM, telegraphed home an appeal for two hundred new workers in the next two years. The stated desire was that most of these would be men who could carry out itinerant evangelism in the more dangerous inland regions. This faith-filled goal was met on time and with the full number of requested workers, though only eighty-four of those were men.

Betty Scott was one of the women who responded to that appeal. She made her application with the CIM during her final year at Moody and was to attend its candidate school in Philadelphia the summer following her graduation. If approved, she would depart for China in the fall.

John, too, felt led to be part of the CIM's forward movement. But he still had another year at Moody plus the whole CIM application and candidate process to complete. By no means was it a given that both John and Betty would indeed end up serving in China under the same mission organization.

In May of 1931 Betty graduated and left Chicago for Philadelphia. John missed her mightily and desired to carry on their relationship immediately via correspondence. Yet he felt an inward constraint not to do so. He simply could not actively promote a relationship that he was not fully sure was within the scope of God's will for his life.

On May 24 he recorded his inner wrestlings in his

journal: "Betty is in Philadelphia now, but I have not been able to write her a letter. After much searching of heart and of the Scriptures, I feel that the Lord would be displeased at my going forward in this direction. And only last week a man came up to my room to have me type a letter for him. A former student, he told me, with tears in his eyes, that he had gotten out of the will of the Lord when he stopped his studies and got married. What grief he has had since. And now, while Betty and I are looking forward to the same field, I cannot move one step in her direction until I am sure that it is the Lord's directive will. I don't want to wreck her life and mine, too."[3]

# *eight*

John's final year at Moody was full of opportunities to further exercise his faith in God. He looked to the Lord to provide him with strength and wisdom to carry out his taxing load of studies, pastoral responsibilities, and part-time work opportunities. In addition, he prayerfully waited on God to supply the finances he could not provide for himself and to give him guidance concerning his relationship with Betty.

Late in the spring of 1931 he picked up some part-time stenographic work. With the income from that, plus a gift of fifty dollars from his father, he was able to make yet another school payment on time.

On June 25 he reflected in his diary: "Praise the Lord for the work. I got a bit behind in my studies, but it taught me some more lessons as to the value of money. When you work good and hard for fifty cents an hour, you do learn something like that. I shall need some more money to get through the term. Praise the Lord for His marvelous provision so far. What is it that makes us so afraid always as to the future? Why can we not learn to trust Him wholly without a shadow of concern for the future?"[1]

On another occasion when John had got down literally to his last nickel, he again experienced God's timely supply for him. He used that final nickel to make an important phone call, which resulted in his needing to make a further call, but now he had no more change. Unsure what to do, John happened to look down and was amazed to see but another nickel in the phone's coin return slot, inadvertently left there by a previous caller.

Of that small but significant instance of providential provision he later said: "Trivial, surely! Only a five-cent piece that somebody had forgotten. But it was there when I needed it, and needed it badly. And God, who knows each sparrow's hopping, knows our little needs too."[2]

John was led to write of such experiences to his missionary brother in Africa: "The Lord has wonderfully taken care of me all through my stay here at Moody's. I count it a great privilege to be here, if only for the lessons I have learned of Him and of His dealings with men. The classroom work is blessed, but I think I have learned even more outside of classes than in them."[3]

That summer Betty completed her missionary candidate training in Philadelphia and was approved to leave for China in the fall. Her picture and a brief testimony appeared in the next issue of *China's Millions*, the CIM's official magazine:

*A missionary's daughter, brought up in China, I have always seen something of heathenism. But, although I knew the Lord as Savior so early that I cannot remember any definite decision, many experiences and battles followed before I truly accepted the Savior as my Lord.*

*During my school years, I prayed that if it were God's will, nothing might prevent me from returning to China as a missionary. My parents and others prayed thus about me, too. I, myself, first made this prayer in 1925 at Keswick, where I received this verse, "For to me to live is Christ, and to die is gain." Since then, other lines of activity, even other fields, have come up before me—and I cannot say they were not of the Lord— while even as recent as September of this year, it was uncertain whether, for physical reasons, I would be accepted at all.*

*But "being in the way, the LORD led me" [Genesis 24:27]. He, who made me willing to serve Him anywhere, has closed all other doors and opened this one—service under the China Inland Mission in China. For this I praise His name; for I love China and believe it is the neediest country—just now, needier than ever.*

*I will make mention of His faithfulness, which is great. Praising the Lord is, I believe, the only thing in the world worth doing. And praising Him involves bringing in other members of His body—those now in heathenism—to Him.[4]*

As Betty traveled across the country in order to sail to China from the West Coast, she was able to spend a day in Chicago with John. They had a wonderful day together, walking by the lake and spending hours talking about their plans for the coming year and beyond.

At the close of the day they attended the Monday evening CIM prayer meeting at the Pages' home. After the meeting they asked to speak privately with Isaac

Page. John, somewhat bashfully, proceeded to divulge to the missionary representative the love that was in his heart for Betty.

"He thought we had not noticed anything!" Page later said.

"Speaking for both of us," John concluded, "we are leaving the matter in the Lord's hands, but feel that He is bringing us together." From the affectionate look in Betty's eyes toward John and the quiet radiance of her expression, Page knew that she readily concurred with his statement.

Around that same time John wrote at length to his father, revealing his thoughts and intentions with regard to Betty:

> *Betty knows that, in all fairness and love to her, I cannot ask her to enter into an engagement with years to wait. But we can have a real understanding, keeping the interests of the Lord's work always first.*
>
> *The China Inland Mission has appealed for men, single men, to itinerate in sections where it would be almost impossible to take a woman, until more settled work has been commenced. Some time ago I promised the Lord that, if fitted for this forward movement, I would gladly go into it, so now I cannot back down without suffi-cient reason, merely upon personal considera-tions. If, after we are out a year or two, we find that the Lord's work would be advanced by our marriage, we need not wait longer.*
>
> *From the way I have written, you and Mother might think that I was talking about a cartload of lumber, instead of something that has dug down*

> *very deep into our hearts. Betty and I have prayed*
> *much about this, and I am sure that, if our sacri-*
> *fice is unnecessary, the Lord will not let us miss*
> *out on any of His blessings. Our hearts are set to*
> *do His will. But this is true, isn't it, our wishes*
> *must not come first? The progress of the Lord's*
> *work is the chief consideration. So there are times*
> *when we just have to stop and think hard.*[5]

Touched by such careful consecration, Peter Stam exclaimed after reading the letter, "Those children are going
to have God's choicest blessing! When God is second,
you will get second best; but when God is really first, you
have His best."

Betty sailed to China where she soon began her language study in the city of Fowyang in northern Anhwei
Province. She was delighted to discover that much of
the Chinese she had learned in earlier years came back
to her, and she was able to make unusually rapid progress
in the language.

At the same time, John sought to remain diligent in
his studies and ministry opportunities in Chicago and
Elida. Before the school year ended, God provided him
with two notable reminders of His faithful provision.

The first involved a blue suit that John's brother Jacob
had given him some months earlier to pass on to any
student at Moody who could use it. For a number of
weeks John unsuccessfully kept an eye out for somebody
the right size who needed a suit. He had about decided to
donate the suit to a local mission, when one evening at a
prayer meeting he spotted a fellow student he had heard
was hard pressed financially.

Privately John told the student about the suit, pur-
posely being nonchalant so as not to risk hurting his pride.

"It just might fit you. If you can make use of it, you're welcome to it."

"Why, that's remarkable!" the young man exclaimed, a smile spreading across his face. "Just this afternoon I started to pray for a suit."

"Of course it fits him!" John noted in his diary that evening.

By the middle of April, just days before his graduation from Moody, John once again found himself completely out of funds. On the way to pick up his own suit that had been mended by a tailor, he stopped at the campus post office to retrieve his mail. He eagerly checked the several letters that had come, thinking that at least one of them might contain a financial gift, but none did.

Continuing on to the tailor, John was embarrassed to have to ask, "Would you mind waiting on the sixty cents I owe you? I'm completely out of cash right now. But I'll be sure to pay you as soon as I'm able."

A short while later that same day John opened a package he had earlier picked up at the post office but had not opened immediately since he supposed it contained no money. Along with its other contents, however, it did include one dollar. With that he had just enough to pay for the repair of the suit plus get a needed haircut.

That night he wrote in his journal, "I won't have a new suit for graduation, but *I'll have the Lord's grace instead, and that's enough!* Hallelujah!"[6]

Three days later, on the morning of April 21, 1932, graduation exercises were held for John's class. Seventy-three students graduated, fifty-one of whom anticipated entering various avenues of vocational Christian service in America and a number of foreign countries. Their eager intent to spread the Gospel was reflected in their class motto, "Bearing Precious Seed." The motto was based on Psalm 126:6 (KJV): "He that goeth forth and weepeth, bearing precious seed, shall doubtless come again with rejoicing, bringing his sheaves with him."

John had the honor of being selected as the male representative from his class to address the graduates and hundreds of guests who gathered for the ceremony. His address, entitled "Go Forward!" (part of which follows), was a stirring challenge to advance the cause of Christ at home and abroad by courageously taking the Gospel to those who otherwise would perish eternally without it.

*Our Lord told us that the field is the world. In politics today men are thinking in terms of international affairs, in business all the continents are being combed for markets, and even in daily life every newspaper reader is becoming world-conscious. And yet we, the people of God, have not fully realized that we are to be a testimony to the world.*

*Heathen populations are growing in numbers daily, but we are not reaching them, much less matching their increasing numbers with increased efforts to bring them the Gospel. Not only are heathen populations growing, but with the frontiers of civilization forging ahead and education advancing, superstition and idolatry are breaking down. Now is the time as never before to reach men whose minds are swept of old barriers ere Communistic Atheism coming in like a flood raises other barriers tenfold harder to level, and before this generation of heathen passes into Christless graves.*

*Our own civilized land also challenges us today as Christian workers. This country once so strong in its Christian testimony is becoming increasingly godless. If the foreign field and the godless civilization about us both call for the faithful planting of divine dynamite that will break stony hearts and save souls, the church of Christ surely has a claim upon our service.*

Turning his attention to the stiff economic challenges that were being experienced by Christian workers during that Great Depression era, John continued:

*If there is a challenge in the work itself, the difficulties under which the work must be done are equally challenging. All forms of Christian work at home and abroad are quite naturally feeling the effect of the depression.*

*Will our God Who once commanded us to preach the Gospel to every nation order a retreat because conditions seem impossible? Let us remind ourselves that the Great Commission was never qualified by clauses that called for advance only if funds were plentiful and if no hardship or self-denial were involved. On the contrary, we were told to expect tribulation and even persecution, but with it victory in Christ.*

*Friends, the challenge of our task with all its attendant difficulties is enough to fill our hearts with dismay. And if we look only to ourselves and to our weaknesses, we are overcome with fore-bodings of defeat. But the answering challenge in our Master's command to go forward should fill*

*us with joy and with the expectation of victory.
He knows our weakness and our lack of supplies;
He knows the roughness of the way, and His
command carries with it the assurance of all we
need for the work. The faithfulness of God is the
only certain thing in the world today, and we
need not fear the result of trusting Him.*

*Our way is plain. We must not retrench in
any work which we are convinced is in His will
and for His glory. We dare not turn back
because the way looks dark. Of this we may be
sure, that if we have been redeemed by Christ's
blood, and are called into His service, His work
done in His way and for His glory will never
lack His support.*

*We, too, must press forward, for it is no time
for delay when a million souls a month pass into
Christless graves in China, with other countries
adding their hundreds of thousands. We must
bring them that message that will deliver them
from the power of Satan and bring them into the
glorious liberty of the children of God.*

*People of God, does it not thrill our hearts
today to realize that we do not answer such a
challenge in our own strength? Think of it! God
Himself is with us as our Captain; the Lord of
Hosts is present in person in every field of con-
flict to encourage us and to fight for us. With
such a Captain, Who never lost a battle, or
deserted a soldier in distress, or failed to get
through the needed supplies, who would not
accept the challenge to "Go forward, bearing
precious seed."*[7]

# *nine*

Shortly after his graduation from Moody, John attended, as Betty had a year earlier, a six-week orientation and training session at the CIM's missionary candidate school in Philadelphia. On July 1, 1932, he was officially approved to serve as a missionary with that organization.

The prospect of proposing marriage to Betty was very much on his mind at that time. An entry in his journal reveals the earnestness with which he was seeking the Lord's leading: "It seems to me that I have been looking too much for some supernatural guidance. It is hard to describe one's feelings, and yet I do have a sense that I am in the way. I have prayed much about this, perhaps more than about any one single thing ever in my life. I have studied my Bible for guidance, and can see no hindrance there at all, if not positive guidance. And circumstances more than point in that direction. May

God frustrate everything if it is not of Him. I do want His will first."[1]

July and August of that year found John back in his hometown of Paterson, making a variety of preparations for his upcoming departure to China. In addition to having his eyes examined and some dental work done, he was admitted to the hospital for surgery that left him weakened and unable to lift heavy loads.

Early in August, while recovering nicely from his surgery, he wrote to Betty, asking if she would consent to marry him someday. He now felt justified in proposing to her since the Lord was obviously leading both of them to serve Him in China under the same mission agency.

With the help of one of his sisters he was able to start shopping for outfit supplies, as well as packing the trunks that would go with him to China. He was also kept busy with opportunities to speak and share his personal testimony at a number of area church services, Sunday school classes, prayer meetings, and Bible study groups.

John had been invited to join a large group of Christian friends on a cruise to Bermuda and other interesting ports of call that summer. He declined, however, explaining, "It might be misunderstood, in light of the privations many missionaries are suffering, if I went on a cruise as luxurious as that one is to be."

On Tuesday, September 8, some forty people gathered at the train station in Paterson to see him off with a time of singing and prayer. The next day he was able to stop and see Niagara Falls. Thursday and Friday he traveled back to Chicago and Elida, Ohio, for send-offs from supporters in both those locations.

Saturday he headed north to Toronto, Canada, for a missions conference there. He spoke at the final service of the conference on Wednesday and again at a combined gathering of the CIM prayer meeting and the Inter-Varsity Christian Fellowship meeting on Friday.

The following week John crossed Canada by rail to Vancouver, British Columbia. Along the way he received a letter from Betty. Apparently she had not received any word from him, including the proposal of marriage that he had written several weeks earlier. "I do hope my letter gets through to her," John wrote in his diary that evening. "However, the will of the Lord be done. I have no good and no desire beyond Him. But I do believe that He will give me Betty on the way."[2]

In recent months Betty had encountered a series of uncertain and disturbing circumstances. First, Henry Ferguson, a missionary to China for thirty-seven years, had been captured by Communist rebels in northern Anhwei Province on May 12. As he was never seen or heard from again, it was later presumed that he had been killed by his captors. Consequently, Betty and the other female missionaries in that part of the province were temporarily moved to the CIM station in Wuhu along the Yangtze River. It was difficult not knowing when they would be able to return or what was happening to the native believers in their absence.

Her parents had written, requesting that she meet them in Shanghai when they returned from furlough early that fall. She eagerly went at the designated time, only to discover that their journey had been postponed. She had not received the message they sent informing her of the change of plans. Disappointed, she went back to Wuhu to await their arrival at a later date. In addition to all this she was puzzled over why she had not heard from John in quite some time.

On Saturday, September 24, John sailed from Vancouver on the *Empress of Japan*. He was delighted to receive thirty-six letters from family members and friends just as the voyage was about to begin. But there was no further correspondence from Betty.

John sailed with five other single young men who were going out with the CIM. They were under the supervision of a returning missionary couple, Mr. and Mrs. Windsor. The missionary party sailed third class, which prompted John to write his parents the following: "I really do praise the Lord that we can go Third Class or Tourist, for while there are probably more comforts in the second class, yet when we realize where all the consecrated money comes from that sends us out, we realize that care must be taken in spending it."[3]

The missionaries soon discovered that there were many different classes of people, spiritually speaking, aboard the ship. Some were fellow Christians who greatly appreciated their efforts at promoting hymn sings and prayer meetings for whoever was interested in participating. Others were unabashed unbelievers who openly scoffed at their efforts to give a positive Christian testimony.

On the first Wednesday of the voyage John was doing some typing in the dining room when he was approached by a Sikh, an adherent of a monotheistic religion of India that had been founded around A.D. 1500. A mixture of Hindu and Islamic belief, the religion was marked by its rejection of idolatry and the caste system. John had noticed the Sikh earlier. A distinguished looking man with his thick black hair, full black beard, and dark turban, he was the head of a sixteen-member party traveling on the ship.

The man, speaking carefully in English, introduced

himself to John and then stated: "I see that you know how to type. Would you be willing to type a letter or two for me tomorrow?"

"Certainly," John said brightly. "I could type them for you yet this evening if you would like."

"I would be grateful."

"You appear to be a religious man," John observed, hoping to strike up a Gospel conversation.

"Oh, yes," the Sikh responded. "I am from India, but I do not practice idolatry as most of my fellow country-men. I have been enlightened so that I follow the One True God."

"I believe in the One True God of the Bible," the young missionary revealed. "In fact, I'm on my way to China as a missionary to tell the people there about Him and His Son, Jesus Christ. Have you ever heard of Jesus?"

"I have heard of the Jesus of Christianity," the man replied honestly, "but I do not know very much about Him."

John was able to share briefly about Christ. Then he offered, "Our Bible teaches much more about Jesus. If I were to give you a copy of our Scriptures, would you read it?"

"I promise that I will," the Sikh answered sincerely. "And I promise that when I arrive back home in India I will send you a copy of our sacred book in exchange."

The next day the ship docked in Honolulu, Hawaii. While attending Moody, John had met a young woman from Honolulu named Ethel Chong. "When you go to China," she told him, "you should surely write and stop in to see me on your way."

He had done just that, thinking that perhaps he would simply meet her family and have a meal with them.

Instead, she and several of her friends greeted them at the dock, and then with three cars took them on a delightful, whirlwind tour of the island. Later in the day they were served a large Chinese dinner by Ethel and her family members.

Then it was off to the University of Hawaii to attend the class in Chinese that their hostess was taking at that time. Mr. Windsor was invited to address the class in Chinese, sharing of his experiences as a missionary in China. That evening they attended a community Bible class at the YWCA. After the Bible lesson was completed, each of the visiting missionaries was invited to share his testimony.

The next morning they reboarded the ship. With the exception of only one day when the sea was, according to John, "quite swelly," the *Empress of Japan* enjoyed smooth sailing conditions throughout the week that followed. Some of the members of his party suffered a bit of seasickness, but he experienced none.

There were representatives from other mission agencies aboard the ship, and all the missionaries started meeting daily for prayer and devotions. They sought to do some evangelistic work among the passengers. John even took the opportunity to witness to three Catholic priests.

On Saturday, October 8, they arrived at Yokohama, Japan. There a letter from Charles Scott awaited John, forewarning him that Betty's outlook on their relationship had seemed reticent in her last letter to her parents. She simply did not know what to make of the fact that she had not heard from John for several weeks.

Charles had visited with John in person near the end of June while he was at CIM candidate training in

Philadelphia. He knew about and heartily approved of John's desire to marry Betty. He also understood the missionary candidate's desire to delay his proposal of marriage until all circumstances made it clear that God was indeed opening the door for him to go to China.

The good doctor rightly supposed that John had written to Betty but that Betty had never received his letters. In the letter that John received at Yokohama, Dr. Scott gave him some fatherly advice on how he might rectify the situation with Betty once he arrived in China.

John and his companions were able to enjoy a day of sightseeing in Yokohama and neighboring Tokyo. A surprise awaited them that evening when they returned to the boat. Some of the loose-living young men who had earlier sneered at them came back aboard the ship with hangovers and deeply depressed following their daylong sinful fling in the city.

"I'm sick of it all," one of the drunken individuals readily confessed to John and his friends when they chanced to meet on deck.

"We truly had a perfectly rotten time of it," another admitted dejectedly.

"I'm beginning to fear myself," a third divulged. "I can see myself slipping, but I can't seem to stop myself." Then he added of the missionaries, "Now you fellows aren't like that. I've noticed that you seem so free."

The opportunity was too good to miss. John and his companions took advantage of it by sharing briefly with the inebriated young men that they, too, could find freedom from sin and true satisfaction in life through faith in Jesus Christ. Unfortunately, their regret was not translated into repentance. Still, John was amazed to realize that the verbal and lifestyle witness he and his fellow missionaries had sought to bear was having some positive effects, even among those who at first had been skeptical.

He later reflected in writing about this "moral freedom" of the missionaries: "And free we are! Not to go into sin; even they didn't enjoy that. But free from sin with the remorse it brings, and able really to enjoy ourselves."[4]

Three days later, on Tuesday, October 11, the *Empress of Japan* approached the coast of China. Miles before the coastline came into view the sea became noticeably dirty, muddied by the tons of silt that the mighty Yangtze River poured into the ocean just past Shanghai. "Twenty miles before we enter the mouth of the river," the ship's steward told John, "one can see the Yangtze mud."

Since it was after ten in the evening when the ship docked at Shanghai, the decision was made to disembark the next day. John went happily to sleep that night knowing that the next morning he would step onto Chinese soil to begin his ministry there.

# *ten*

John was up early the next morning and out on deck, eager to catch glimpses of life in China. The first thing he saw was a tiny Chinese houseboat anchored right below the deck on which he stood. The craft, about seven feet wide and twenty feet long, was the permanent home of a family of four.

The mother was busy cooking the family's breakfast over a small fire in the bottom of the boat. Needing to clean a dish, she tied a rag to a rope, dipped it into the dirty harbor water, pulled it up again, and wiped out the bowl. Her little girl was already out of bed and needed to wash. The youngster lowered another rag into the muddy river, and then used it to scrub her face and feet. The family's young teenage son, who had been sleeping on the deck with a small white dog, roused himself. Rolling up his blankets, he handed them to his mother who, in turn, stored them under the deck.

John looked at the impoverished family and around at a number of beggars who dotted the wharf. "Here I am dressed in good European clothes and doubtless appearing to them like a regular millionaire," he thought to himself. "But how can I best help them and the millions of others like them in China? Not by just handing out in a hurry the few dollars I have in my pockets. There are doubtless so many poor people and beggars here in China that thousands of dollars would not suffice to give every one ever so little help. No, it is not money. Money would only help them for a little while and then they will be poor again. It is the Gospel of Christ alone that can help them."

Less than forty-eight hours after arriving in Shanghai, John would write home to his family more of his initial impressions:

> *I have seen people huddled together; men wearing next to nothing, and that pretty well in rags; faces that look full of suffering and sorrow; children with ugly-looking sores on their heads; miserable-looking eating places.*
>
> *May the Lord give us indeed to see a far deeper and a far worse spiritual need: a soul that is starved and about ready to pass out into eternity, an eternity of darkness; a life clad in rags instead of in the garments of righteousness; men that are putrifying sores from head to foot in the sight of a living God. May the Lord show us their spiritual need, nor ever let us get so accustomed to poverty and suffering as to become insensible to another's need and no longer to have His heart of love that yearned over all men's troubles.[1]*

At nine a small steamer called a tender transported the missionaries to the customs dock. There they were met by a missionary and a Chinese helper from the CIM mission home. After clearing customs, the new arrivals were taken to the CIM's spacious residence in Shanghai's international settlement. A glorious surprise awaited John there that he would not have dared to hope for: Betty Scott was in Shanghai and he could see her that very day!

Since last writing to him, she had made a second trip to Shanghai to meet her parents when they arrived from America. After that an infection of her tonsils requiring treatment by a doctor made it necessary for her to travel to the coastal city a third time that fall. She was still there when John arrived.

When the couple met that day, any doubt concerning how they both truly felt was quickly dispelled. Betty learned of the letter proposing marriage that John had mailed more than two months earlier but she had never received. He immediately assured her that his deep affection for her had never ceased and that he wholeheartedly desired to marry her.

He explained that the only reason he had delayed in writing the marriage proposal as long as he had was his desire to make sure that he was acting in concert with the Lord's clear leading and not just out of natural human impulse. Now that God had led both of them to serve in the same country and under the same missionary agency, John felt complete freedom to ask for the cherished desire of his heart—her hand in marriage.

Betty's heart, in turn, overflowed with sheer relief and gratitude. Instead of facing further uncertainty over how their relationship stood or, worse yet, the trauma of discovering that John's feelings for her had changed, she now clearly saw that God was indeed bringing her together with the man whom she had come to love so dearly. With wonder and joy she accepted his proposal that day, this time offered in person rather than by letter.

At the end of that first dramatic day in China, John wrote in his journal: "October 12, 1932— Hallelujah! Wonders never will cease. Our Heavenly Father so arranged it that Betty was here in Shanghai instead of being away up in northern Anhwei. She had to have tonsil tissue removed and was told to come on down for that. And she has promised to be my wife. How I do praise the Lord for all His ordering and arranging. He will not fail those who wait for Him."[2]

The young couple immediately announced their engagement to their fellow missionaries, who readily shared in their joy. John reported to his family by letter: "Everybody about the mission was so kind and so sympathetic, too. You'd almost think they ought to have their doubts about a new missionary just coming out getting engaged right off the bat, but not a few of them noticed the coincidence of Betty being down here just at the right time."[3]

A missionary from Australia asked him, "How did you two work it that you were able to meet here in Shanghai?"

"That's what's so blessed," John responded. "We didn't work it at all. It was totally unplanned and unexpected. The Lord brought it all about."

Another missionary teased, "I think you ought to pay Betty's doctor bill, since you are the one who is gaining the benefit of her staying here."

Mr. Gibb, the CIM's field director in China, told John: "I don't see any reason at all why you shouldn't plan on getting married just as soon as your first year of service is completed. Of course, as you know, there is a mandatory one-year waiting period for all our new missionaries who become engaged."

John and Betty were able to spend six days together in Shanghai. During that time they ventured into the city and purchased a simple gold wedding band for Betty from a reputable jeweler. Since they did not know exactly when and where they would get married, or if they would be anywhere near a jeweler at the time of their wedding, they thought it best to select the ring ahead of time.

John desired to get Betty a diamond ring, but she refused, saying, "Sometimes it might be a hindrance when we're working among the really poor here in China. And no one will be put out by my not wearing a diamond."

"But won't you sometimes regret not having one?" John queried.

"Oh, I might be embarrassed a bit about it once in awhile," she admitted. "But on the whole I think it's best that I not."

On Sunday they enjoyed attending the children's service at the Door of Hope Mission. There they witnessed two to three hundred girls, ranging in age from toddlers to young teens, all dressed in matching pants and short coats, happily singing Christian hymns and choruses in both Chinese and English. Especially impressive to the young missionaries was the way in which the girls were able to recite Scriptures they had committed to memory.

Many of these girls had been slaves, literally, before being rescued and turned over to the mission by the Chinese courts. One of the mission's brightest pupils had been taken from an opium-smoking mistress who was in the habit of severely beating her. The young girl lived at the mission for some time before she could truly believe that the unconditional love she experienced was genuine. At the mission she would never experience the abuse that had always been a part of her life.

On Tuesday morning, October 18, Betty left Shanghai to return to Fowyang. Along with Mr. and Mrs. Glittenberg, recent appointees to that same city in northwestern Anhwei Province, she would travel first by train and then by bus.

That same Tuesday evening John and a few other young men boarded a steamer to make the three-day trip up the Yangtze to Anking, in southeastern Anhwei, where they would spend several months in language school. He would not see Betty again for a full year.

# *eleven*

The steamer bearing John and his missionary companions arrived at Anking after dark on Friday, October 21. Two veteran missionaries were there to welcome the new arrivals. A native teacher at the CIM language school, Yen Hsien Seng, had traveled with John's party on the boat.

Mr. Yen made it his habit to meet every boat that brought new students to the school. A man of influence with coolies and customs officials, he could arrange for coolies to carry luggage to the compound much less expensively than the missionaries. As often happened, he was able to get John and his companions through customs without their needing to open a single box. He also convinced the guards at the city gate, which had already been closed and barred for the night, to admit the contingent of missionaries.

It took the group half an hour to walk across Anking,

the capital city of Anhwei Province, to the CIM compound. They made their way, mainly uphill, along narrow, stone-slabbed streets that were more like stairs than roads. Eventually they arrived at the mission premises, a large complex more than one hundred yards square, which was completely surrounded by high stone walls. The compound included a church building, separate missionary and native living quarters, a school, and an athletic field.

The next day John got settled into his new room and then took a walk. Due to some anti-foreign sentiment in Anking, students at the language school were generally not allowed to walk through the city. Just a couple of minutes from the compound, however, was the city's north gate and from there students could exit for a walk in the country. Rolling foothills overlooking the Yangtze surrounded the city, and several miles in the distance mountains could be seen.

As John walked along he saw women cleaning their laundry beside streams and ponds. Most of the women followed the ancient Chinese custom of foot binding. Tiny feet were considered desirable for Chinese women, so from early girlhood females had their feet tightly wrapped. This custom literally stunted the natural growth of the feet and eventually crippled the women. To relatives back home John wrote: "It's pitiful to see these poor women, some of them under heavy loads, trying to hobble along on their bound feet that are little more than stumps."

He also observed small children out in the fields, raking grass together and tying it into bundles. The bundles were then swung over carrying poles and transported by the children to their homes where the grass was burned as fuel. Again, he wrote in a letter: "But with all their heavy loads, and you'll see the little fellows just staggering along in their little dogtrot fashion, they are still a cheery bunch. I can almost always get a smile from them. Yesterday I stepped aside in the narrow path between rice fields to let three little lads pass and the last one pulled up his hand in salute. They surely are likeable little people."[1]

John was astounded at the number of graves on the hills outside the city walls. Everywhere he walked, grave mounds could be seen, often one right on top of another. He was also amazed at the low level of respect with which these graves were treated. Walking paths sometimes ran over the tops of graves. Years earlier and in more recent times, deep trenches had been dug all around the city to assist in defending against various rebel attacks. These plowed right through the middle of any graves that stood in the way.

Furthermore, coffins were not always buried immediately. Numerous coffins could be seen set out around the hillsides, simply covered with reed mats. One of Anking's veteran missionaries divulged to the new arrivals, "Around here you are likely to hear that some man wants to bury his wife. And then you'll likely as not find out that she has been dead for years!"

As John looked out over the seemingly countless graves, he reflected soberly to himself. "How many of these people will see the light at the Resurrection of the just? Surely not many. Why has the church of Christ been so slow in discharging its duty to the Chinese?"

In addition to these sights, John immediately picked up on a whole array of new sounds that were a regular part of life in Anking. At six each morning a chorus of bugles (blown by soldiers) announced the arrival of the new day. Then, not long after that, the squealing of pigs could be heard off in the distance. About one hundred pigs were slaughtered every day to help feed the city's one hundred thousand inhabitants. There were other sounds, though, that were not so benign. Once in his opening weeks at Anking John heard a volley of gunshots ring out shortly after dawn just outside the city wall as a number of Communist rebels were executed by firing squad.

During the day a cacophony of sounds was heard throughout the city. Vendors drew attention to their wares by beating drums, beggars announced their presence by tinkling bells, wheelbarrows with their ungreased wheels squeaked along in protest under heavy loads, and women slapped and pounded their wet laundry on cleaning boards. Sometimes a woman could be heard wailing for hours, grieving the death of a family member or some other tragedy. During celebrations, great or small, fire-crackers were often heard. These sounds awakened within John many senses all at once.

Twenty-three single men from eight countries attended the language school that year: four British; four Germans; three Swedes; one Norwegian; three Australians; two New Zealanders; three Canadians; and three from the United States. The day new missionaries arrived in Anking from England, Germany, and Sweden, John wrote in his diary: "May the Lord keep us in blessed harmony together and teach us many lessons of His grace."[2]

Language study got underway on Monday, October 24. A regimented schedule was followed Monday through Friday:

6:00 A.M.   Rising bell

| 7:30 | Breakfast |
|---|---|
| 8:00–8:20 | English prayers |
| 8:30–9:00 | Chinese prayers |
| 9:00–12:00 | Classes and study |
| 12:30 P.M. | Dinner |
| 1:45–4:00 | Classes and study |
| 4:00–5:30 | Exercise |
| 5:30 | Supper |
| 6:00–6:20 | Prayer for CIM workers in the provinces |
| 7:00–8:00 | Study |
| 10:00 | Lights out |

At the morning English prayers session a different student each day would share a brief meditation as they made their way through John's Gospel together. After completing a handful of elementary Chinese lessons, the students also attended the Chinese prayers session each morning, straining to pick up on the meaning of the hymns, prayers, or devotions that were being shared by and with the natives.

John especially enjoyed the morning language class taught by Mr. Yen. The skilled instructor, employing only vocabulary words the students were studying in their lessons, could talk at great length, telling Bible stories, spinning yarns, explaining local customs, and describing scenes from China or various foreign cities such as New York or London.

"One minute he'll be mimicking an ox in trying to make us get the meaning of that character," John described Mr. Yen to relatives. "Then he'll be in a hospital bed suffering from tuberculosis (you can imagine what that would be like). Then it will be a feast with the menu of pig, chicken, duck, etc., drawn on the board.

93

From that he'll go on to illustrate how chairs and tables have no understanding, but men do. And by way of diversion, he'll tell us how dogs can understand too, illustrating it by making himself to act the part of the dog, wagging tail and all. It's just a howl all the way through, but gives us good practice in the spoken language."

In the afternoon the students met individually with a native teacher to read through whole sections of Chinese literature. They took care to follow their tutor in reproducing sounds and tones as closely as they could. Of this complex and often confusing process John said: "It's amazing how these teachers will pick you up on a wrong tone in which we English-speaking people can hear hardly any difference. We seem quite utterly oblivious of this tone business unless we listen very, very carefully, but these Chinese pick out the difference in intonation very quickly."[3]

After each full day of exacting, intensive study the students welcomed the opportunity to get out-of-doors for some refreshing exercise. This they did virtually every weekday, even after the weather turned cold and wet. Their favorite recreation was a type of basketball played out on the compound's athletic field. A description in one of John's letters makes it sound like the games sometimes resembled football more than basketball: "Our Anking brand of basketball involves pulling, tugging, pushing, etc. It's a good, clean, fast game, and fairly open, but of course there is a lot of fast running and jumping and you get thrown down."[4] John was under doctor's orders not to exert himself strenuously until six months after his surgery of the previous summer, so at first he was unable to compete in the basketball games. However, he was able to participate and get plenty of exercise by serving as referee.

Weekends provided the students with a welcome break from their taxing schedule of classes and studies. Friday evenings they met by themselves as a group for informal prayer and encouragement. They had Saturday afternoons free. John often used his discretionary time on the weekend to get caught up on his considerable correspondence to relatives and friends and to take a walk in the country. On Saturday evenings a different student each week shared his personal testimony. Sundays were devoted to worship and relaxation. They attended a Chinese service in the morning and had their own English service in the evening where again students took turns bringing the message.

Just how much of a strain each week of study was—and what a relief the weekends were—can be gauged by some of the remarks which John made in his journal on various Saturdays or Sundays: "Another week gone. Praise God for these weekends with their Lord's day rest"; "Praise God for the day of rest. Another day spent with Him"; "Praise God for all His great goodness. I do love these weekends of rest and refreshment"; "A very blessed day today with the Word and the Lord. Had a good walk this afternoon"; "Praise God for another weekend with its chance to draw a breath"; "The week is done, and I am glad."[5]

John was determined to maintain close fellowship with the Lord despite the demanding schedule he faced. He worked hard at safeguarding a period of time each morning and evening to devote to personal Bible reading and prayer. Several diary entries reveal the desire he had to be close to God:

Oct. 28—Oh, that I may stay close to the Lord. It is so easy to live on the past or just in hope of the future.

Nov. 2—Am succeeding in having some blessed times with the Word, the Lord enabling me to spend 1 and 1/2 hours or more each day in my devotions.

Nov. 4—May the Lord keep me, with all this busyness, very close to Him.

Nov. 12—Gave my testimony tonight. It's rather late and I've not yet had all my time with the Lord. It's getting to be a bit of a fight to keep time out for Him. Oh, to know Him better.

Dec. 14—Praise the Lord for good studies. But, oh, to see His power in all my life.[6]

Betty, too, was never long out of John's thoughts. He eagerly looked for her weekly letters and was sharply disappointed when, as happened more than once, they were delayed by faulty mail service.

Her letters both thrilled and concerned him. They brought news of a remarkable moving of God's Spirit in the area where she was ministering and related exciting initial opportunities she was having among the natives. But Betty's letters also told of significant dangers.

# *twelve*

Fowyang, where Betty went after parting from John in Shanghai, was located 175 miles northwest of Anking. That section of Anhwei Province was different from the area in which John was staying. Anking was surrounded by wet rice fields and green rolling hills, while Fowyang was bordered by dry wheat fields and brown flat plains.

But despite the arid landscape, showers of spiritual blessings had come to northern Anhwei Province in recent years. For a number of years prior to that, missionaries had served in and around Fowyang with little fruit, and in 1927 all missionaries were forced to evacuate due to the tumultuous political circumstances and the threatening antiforeign sentiment in the area. The missionaries were deeply concerned about the welfare of the small band of relatively new believers whom they had left behind. Would they remain strong in their faith despite the Communist persecution they were facing?

When the missionaries were able to return, however, they were astounded to discover that the Chinese church in that area had not only survived but had actually thrived during their absence. In spite of much persecution, the native Christians had boldly shared their faith, resulting in scores of people being won to Christ.

In Fowyang, rather than needing to gather a few disheartened believers, the missionaries found a congregation of 250 regular attenders! A baptismal service was held shortly after the missionaries' return in which eleven men and fifteen women publicly confessed their faith in Jesus Christ. Eighty professing believers took part in the communion service that followed.

A spirit of revival pervaded the entire region. In an outstation thirty miles from Fowyang, where the Christians were on fire for Christ notwithstanding persecution, seventy-one men and women were examined by the missionaries and church leaders and accepted for baptism. New groups of earnest young Christians sprang up in various towns and villages. There was a pressing need for teachers to work with the many new believers. One missionary, a Mr. Costerus, testified of the Christians in two villages where fairly large congregations were meeting: "None of them knows much of the Gospel. About all they can do, when they come together, is to sing and pray. But the Lord is working among them. They are spoken of as 'wild sheep' at present, because there is nobody to care for them."

By the fall of 1932 the work in Fowyang was being carried out by three missionaries: Mr. and Mrs. Hamilton and Miss Nancy Rodgers. As it was time for the Hamiltons to go on furlough, Mr. and Mrs. Glittenberg, having served elsewhere in China, were appointed to take their place. Fowyang's three veteran missionaries, overwhelmed with the work that needed to be done throughout the district, gladly welcomed the Glittenbergs, Betty, and another single missionary, Katie Dodd.

Although Betty had further language study to complete, because of her ability to understand and speak some Chinese already, she had the opportunity to engage in ministry shortly after her arrival in Fowyang. Only a couple of weeks after coming there she, along with Katie and a native Bible woman, Miss Liu, set out on a short evangelistic itineration. (Bible women were female evangelist-teachers who worked especially with women and children.) Traveling in a southeasterly direction, they followed the main road that was not far from the Hwang Ho River. In a letter to one of her brothers Betty described the dry, desolate scenery they encountered along the way:

> *Anhwei is the flattest country you ever saw in your life. It's almost like the ocean when very calm, with only here and there a bunch of trees and houses which can't be seen far off, as the houses are mud and the trees dusty, like everything else. Sometimes the first we saw of a homestead was the bunch of brilliant red peppers, hanging up to dry against a wall. These and the persimmon trees, which have a glorious way of turning color so that every leaf is a different hue, ranging from all oranges and reds to green, were almost the only bits of live color that we saw all day.*
>
> *Everywhere the people were harvesting sweet potatoes, out of what looked like piles of dry dust. Whenever a little donkey trotted by, it*

*raised a cloud of dust that could be seen for*
*miles. Sometimes we were beside the river,*
*which was almost blue, and had cut deep banks*
*for itself out of dry cliffs.[1]*

The women were transported by rickshaws that had inflatable rubber tires. These tires were thin and well worn and had been wrapped with strips of cloth to try to prevent punctures. The rickshaw men moved along the bumpy road at a very slow pace, stopping now and again to pick burrs off the tires.

In the middle of the afternoon the party stopped at a market town for dinner. Flies swarmed everywhere, landing indiscriminately on people and produce alike. The travelers made their way to the local inn, a mud house, where they were shown to a small inner room. The townspeople crowded in after them, eager to observe these foreign women.

The landlady pushed the curious onlookers out of the room, exclaiming crossly in a loud voice, "Out! Out, all of you. Give the ladies some privacy. They are only human beings like you yourselves are."

Good-naturedly, however, a number of the people sneaked back into the room until they stood three deep all around the group of guests. The visiting evangelists took advantage of the situation by sharing a brief Gospel testimony. Miss Liu did most of the talking while Betty and Katie distributed tracts.

Still hoping to gain a degree of privacy for her guests, the landlady made an excuse to transfer them to a back courtyard. There she hurried them into another little room.

"Firmly closing the door," Betty reported later, "she left us to our meal with chopsticks in almost total darkness, not even able to see whether we were eating any of the flies! Such of the crowd as were already in before the door was shut gleamed at us with shining eyes."

After dinner they traveled on to another village, Hsingchitzi, where they spent the night. Being a CIM outstation, there was a small chapel there. The friendly local Christians brought the weary travelers hot water and boiled peanuts as well as other items to make their stay as comfortable as possible. Betty and Katie intended to sleep in the loft above the chapel, but the presence of rats bothered Katie, so she took her bedding down the ladder and slept on chapel benches. "I heard the rats," Betty said afterward, "but was too sleepy to haul my bedding down a rickety ladder, and resolved not to move since nothing had scampered over me yet."

The next day, a Friday, they continued on to Yingshan, a rather large city where the CIM had another outstation. The city wall could be seen for miles as they approached from across the plain. No missionary had ever lived in the city, even though the nearby district had experienced a marked moving of God's Spirit, and it was hoped that Betty and Katie would soon be able to move there to carry on a ministry to the city's thousands of women and children.

The CIM premises in Yingshan were located back away from the main streets. A lovely round moon gate led into the inner courtyard. A native evangelist, Mr. Yang, lived with his large family in the main residence there. Betty, Katie, and Miss Liu stayed in the guest room that was right beside the main gate, between it and the chapel.

"How the people *streamed* in yesterday afternoon after our arrival!" Betty wrote to John from Yingshan. "They were in the chapel which is almost all open, in the court,

101

and in our room, although we tried to keep them out of the last mentioned. And there were the loveliest young girls, besides crowds of women, young students, and children.

"We gave out many tracts, and the Bible woman was talking almost every minute. Katie and I would attempt a few words here and there. I counted fifty or sixty at one time, and they kept coming and going. We invited all back for Sunday to hear the preaching service, and how we long to start Bible study classes for these educated girls, and other classes to teach the illiterate women and the children the Bible!"

Mr. Yang led three church services at the chapel on Sunday. In addition, a special children's meeting was held in the afternoon. All through the day the mission compound was crowded with people. Betty and Katie worked with the children and distributed tracts to them while Miss Liu preached to group after group of women. By day's end the small missionary band had distributed well over half of the three thousand pieces of literature they had brought along on the trip.

Of the children who attended the meetings Betty wrote: "Some among them were the most precious little children you ever saw—really lovable, unspoiled ones, whose eyes just shone, and who crowded round us and repeated every word we said, every verse and chorus, line by line, for hours. There was no such thing as rushing in late for Sunday school, and rushing home again right afterward. They did go home for meals, but not all at the same time! They weren't fresh and cheeky either; they were simply interested and thrilled. All of them wanted us to come back later and live in the city, and teach them the Bible."[2]

The next day Katie became ill and they decided to

return to Fowyang by sailing on a boat up the river, thinking that would be a quicker and more comfortable mode of travel. After two days of battling contrary winds, however, they needed to abandon that plan and again hire rickshaws. They were considerably delayed along the remainder of the way by a number of tire punctures and finally arrived in Fowyang after the city gates had been closed for the night. Thankfully, the gates were opened for them so they did not need to spend the night outside the city walls.

A short while after they returned, the annual autumn conference was held in Fowyang. The conference was a tremendous blessing, with over eight hundred people in attendance. Eighty-two Chinese were baptized that fall. One of those, an elderly man in his eighties, had a wayward son who had caused him much concern.

The day the father returned home from his baptism the son emphatically declared, "It will never do for the two of us to live in the same house now!"

"But why?" the old man asked, taken aback by the unexpected remark.

"Because you're a Christian now and I'm not."

"But why don't you join me in becoming a Christian?"

"No, it's too late for that. I'm too deep in sin to be saved."

"It's never too late to come to the Savior, my son. Just look at your old father." The son was still not convinced, so the elderly gentleman said, "Surely you can at least be prayed for. Let me call for some of the leaders of the church to come and pray with you."

The son agreed, and the church elders were summoned. They were able to share the Gospel with the young man who, in turn, surrendered to Christ and was gloriously saved from his life of sin.

103

# *thirteen*

There were many blessings, but the Fowyang missionaries experienced marked dangers and difficulties as well that fall. Less than a week after Betty and her companions returned from Yingshan, the Glittenbergs' baby daughter, Lois, became seriously ill with dysentery. Mrs. Glittenberg set out with her infant for the nearest hospital, which was a long day's journey away by bus in Hwaiyuan.

Along the way, however, the bus was stopped by a band of rebel soldiers. "Everyone off the bus!" they commanded.

As she stepped off the bus, Mrs. Glittenberg held tightly to Lois and a small handbag that contained the baby's medicine and a few other personal items. The soldiers began going from passenger to passenger, taking whatever luggage they had. When they approached the missionary and reached for the handbag, she pleaded with them in Chinese. "Please don't take that. All it contains is medicine for my baby, who is very sick. I'm taking her to the hospital in Hwaiyuan. Without the medicine she might die."

Unconcerned about this foreign woman or her baby, the soldiers confiscated and opened the handbag. Finding a large bottle of medicine, they opened it. Smelling the alcohol the strong medicine contained, three of the soldiers drank the entire bottle on the spot. After that they refused to return the bag.

A few minutes later the rebels filed onto the bus and drove away, leaving all the passengers to fend for themselves. After considerable delay, rickshaws were located to transport the passengers to their desired destinations.

Fortunately, Mrs. Glittenberg had sewn some money into the hem of her dress and was able to use that to hire a rickshaw. She continued on to the hospital but the long delay proved fatal. Baby Lois, with her head of darling golden curls, died at the hospital of dysentery. The Glittenbergs were, of course, deeply saddened over the loss of their infant. But their faith in God and their determination to serve Him faithfully in the place where He had called them remained unshaken.

The sentiment Betty expressed in a letter immediately after this tragedy expressed the faith-filled outlook of the Glittenbergs and other committed missionaries with whom she was associated at that time: "Here in this work, you just have to trust everything to God, including your children, and know that He will do exactly what is best, and according to His will."[1]

Weeks later the missionaries at Fowyang again had occasion to lean on the Lord through a threatening circumstance. On Sunday, December 11, Betty stayed home from the Chinese church service to check in on Mrs.

Glittenberg who was tending to her young son, Milton. The boy had been ill since the death of his sister and was beginning to develop the measles.

Around two that afternoon two government soldiers suddenly entered the courtyard of the CIM compound and sat down, obviously intending to stay. They were scouts who had been sent ahead to find a suitable place for a larger contingent of soldiers to stay when it arrived later.

The cook was the only man in the house at the time, all the others still being at the lengthy native worship service that had not yet dismissed. He went out to tell the soldiers that they and their companions would not be able to set up quarters there. One of the soldiers became angry and struck the cook, who then rushed off to the church to get the gatekeeper and Mr. Wang, the teacher at the compound's school for girls.

Betty ventured out to speak with the soldiers herself. "I'm sorry that we won't be able to assist you," she said politely, "but our buildings here are all in use. You see, we have a girls' school, our missionary residence, and a few other rooms that are already occupied by various people who work here."

The cook, gatekeeper, and teacher returned shortly to speak further with the soldiers, who remained unmoved. Not long after that the church service ended, and the girls returned to the two-storied building that contained their classrooms downstairs and their dormitory on the second floor. Minutes later, two companies of soldiers, composed of some sixty men, arrived at the compound and entered the downstairs of the girls' school. In no time they had moved all the desks and tables out into the courtyard.

Mr. Glittenberg was away in Shanghai where he was picking up his older children from boarding school so they could spend Christmas vacation together as a family. A local native evangelist, Mr. Ho, spoke with the individuals who seemed to be in charge of the newly arrived soldiers. Getting nowhere, he went to the local yamen to appeal to the city magistrate.

That official was completely obliging to the evangelist. Hearing that the soldiers had entered a girls' school, he immediately responded, "It is not proper for the men to remain there. I shall see to it that they are off the premises by three o'clock."

The missionaries and native Christians were heartened by Mr. Ho's report but continued to pray earnestly about the situation. They knew full well that the local official could easily change his mind. If he met with resistance from the tired soldiers, who doubtless would be less than excited about having to move again, he could easily conjure up excuses for his sudden change of heart. The small group of Christian workers became even more concerned when the soldiers began to peer around into the school's kitchen and even into the rooms on the second floor where Nancy Rodgers and the girls lived.

Even as the believers were continuing in fervent prayer, they heard a sharp whistle and some commands being given. When they looked out they discovered the soldiers were lined up at attention, in a long double line that stretched from the door of the school to the courtyard gate. A short while later they marched out in orderly fashion, so that by 4:00 P.M. not a single soldier remained on the compound.

"We all went grinning around in a sort of joyful daze," Betty related afterward, "and praising the mercy

107

of God not a few times. Evidently these soldiers are out after local bandits. There have been increasingly more [soldiers] lately."[2]

John, in writing to his parents of this incident, commented further: "I was especially glad to see the calm way in which Betty was taking all of these happenings. I do praise God for her. But the above will help you pray more intelligently for her and for us both when we get out into the work. One never knows what we may get into, but of course, we do know the Lord Jehovah reigns. Above all, don't let anything worry you about us."

He then shared a poem he had just received from Charles Scott. The poem, entitled "Afraid?" was written by Presbyterian missionary E. H. Hamilton following the recent martyrdom of one of his colleagues, J. W. Vinson, at the hands of rebel soldiers in northern China. A small Chinese girl who escaped from the bandits related the incident that provided the inspiration for Hamilton's poem.

"Are you afraid?" the bandits asked Vinson as they menacingly waved a gun in front of him.

"No," he replied with complete assurance. "If you shoot, I go straight to heaven."

His decapitated body was found later.

Afraid? Of What?
To feel the spirit's glad release?
To pass from pain to perfect peace,
The strife and strain of life to cease?
    Afraid—of that?

Afraid? Of What?
Afraid to see the Savior's face,

To hear His welcome, and to trace
The glory gleam from wounds of grace?
    Afraid—of that?

    Afraid? Of What?
A flash, a crash, a pierced heart;
Darkness, light, O Heaven's art!
A wound of His a counterpart!
    Afraid—of that?

    Afraid? Of What?
To do by death what life could not—
Baptize with blood a stony plot,
Till souls shall blossom from the spot?
    Afraid—of that?

John concluded the letter: "And so we can praise God that for us everything is well. If we should go on before, it is only the quicker to enjoy the bliss of the Savior's presence, the sooner to be released from the fight against sin and Satan. Meanwhile, we can continue to praise Him from whom all blessings flow."[3]

# *fourteen*

ince the days of its founder, Hudson Taylor, the CIM had annually designated December 31 as a day of prayer for all its missionaries. John's journal reveals that he eagerly anticipated that special time of extended communion with the Lord as 1932 drew to a close:

"December 30—A good day of study today. All mail has been answered. Now I look forward to tomorrow, the day of prayer, and the next day, Sunday, two days set aside specially for the Lord. Oh, Lord, make Thyself more real than ever to us. In Jesus' Name, Amen."[1]

By the middle of January 1933, the weather had turned very cold. John awoke several mornings to discover that the water in the washbasin in his unheated room had frozen over. The students spent considerable time congregated in the kitchen-dining room where the wood-burning cooking stove was located. They also had small kerosene heaters that they used sparingly to help combat the cold.

In describing these conditions to his relatives, John made it clear that he was not seeking pity: "But if you hear anybody saying, 'Poor John,' just you stop it right away. We've just been full of praise to God here for good health and good spirits. And with all the discomforts of cold rooms, etc., I'd far rather be here in the Lord's will than at home in nice warm houses with hot and cold water, etc. I've just been amazed how well I have been keeping. I've hardly even had a cold."[2]

Many nights before climbing into bed he pulled on the pair of heavy wool socks he had bought in Chicago after discovering the much-needed five-dollar bill on Michigan Avenue. The socks served as a nightly reminder to him of God's faithfulness.

John was also encouraged as he continued to make progress in learning the Chinese language. After attending the Chinese church service on Sunday, January 15, he wrote in his diary, "Enjoyed Mr. Yen's sermon today and was much pleased to be able to understand so much of it."[3]

The services at the native church were full of features that fascinated the new missionary. A month earlier, before he started understanding a bit more Chinese, John had included a colorful description of the services in one of his letters home:

*The church itself is a plain building in the front of this compound with plain wooden benches and nothing at all ornate about it. It has Scripture texts carved in wooden boards here and there.*

*As you go into the church you first notice that the men and women are separated, the women sitting on the left facing the pulpit and*

*the men on the right. They come in all dressed
up in their many garments, the number depending upon the coldness of the day. You'd be interested to notice how the men mostly wear gowns
over their trouser effects, while very many of the
women wear trousers and a short coat that ends
just about at the hips, quite reversing our styles
at home. It's quite all right to wear your cap in
church, although we foreigners don't, and it's
quite the thing to be wearing one of those little
skull caps with a small button on the top.*

*Of course there's no heat. The men don't use
foot warmers in church, but the women bring
them along. The foot warmers of the cheaper
kind are just a clay pot with a handle in the middle. You put your feet on both sides of the handle.
The pot is filled with fire, probably of charcoal,
and covered over with ashes to conserve the heat.
The more expensive kinds are heavy brass affairs
with brass grates on top and handles that swing
off to the side and out of the way. It's funny to see
a woman take her brass foot warmer, put it on
the seat beside her, then warm her hands for
awhile. Perhaps she'll pull over some of her
wadded coat and put it over the warmer to get
the benefit of the heat there too.*

*The hymn being announced, we foreigners do
a good deal of hunting to find where it is and
then follow it closely, singing the characters we
know, and preserving more or less silence when
we get to those we don't know. Betty says that it's
rather interesting to hear the singing in Fowyang.
Here Mr. or Mrs. Whipple play the organ while
the singing is going on, but there they have no*

*one to play the organ and no real singer to lead
off. So the whole church full, some six hundred of
them [in Fowyang], sing away, and sometimes
the front of the church will finish a whole verse
or so ahead of the back of the church.*

*When it comes to prayer we all rise for that
and those who wear glasses take them off as a
sign of respect. When we take communion, too,
we rise out of our seats to receive the elements.
It's considered the respectful thing to do.*

*We have the collection next. The dear old dea-
con stands up and reads off the list of what the
people have given, or promised to give, and then
perhaps finishes off by telling the people that it
isn't enough. Then the pastor hands them the big
red wooden plates and they go around getting the
collection, most of which is in big copper coins,
much bigger than our pennies at home. The people put them on in little piles. Some of them put
theirs up in nice little white bags.*

*Then comes the sermon. Not understanding
much of the sermons, I can't tell you much of
their manner and content, but will mention that
it is quite interesting to watch the faces of the
foreigners as they listen. Although you know
they are getting only an occasional word, yet
you will see almost every one listening with as
rapt attention as though he were listening to a
wonderful sermon at home as we strain to get
just a little of the message. Such rows of earnest
faces one seldom sees.*

*After prayer and the benediction we are dis-
missed. You can see the Chinese wrapping up their
hymnbooks and Bibles (for they all bring their*

*own) in handkerchief affairs, then going off to the
guest room to drink tea or to their own homes.*

*One is quite conscious, despite all these dif-
ferences, that he is in the house of God. You may
see some Chinese woman spitting on the floor. Or
in the middle of the summertime, they tell me, you
may see somebody get up right in the middle of
the sermon to fan the seat which has been getting
a bit hot. Nevertheless, this is the house of God,
and these people have come to worship Him.[4]*

John made special mention in another letter of a
mother, Mrs. Hsieh, and her evangelist son who were
prominent members in the Anking congregation. In earlier
years, while living in another province, their family fell
upon hard times and, as a result, Mrs. Hsieh was to be sold
into slavery. The son, however, volunteered and was sold
in her place. Sometime later he learned that his mother had
been sold as a slave by his father. Running away from his
master, Hsieh searched for his mother and finally suc-
ceeded in finding her in Anhwei Province. There they both
came to faith in Christ.

Possessing a strong and striking personality, Hsieh
developed into a prominent evangelist who ministered in
most of the provinces of China. A mighty man of God,
he was greatly used to stir up Christians and to bring
conviction upon them.

Of Mrs. Hsieh, John testified: "She is a most happy
soul. There she comes in her old padded garments and
bound feet, coming to almost all the meetings and regularly to morning prayers, bringing her Bible and hymnbook and reading out her verse when her turn comes.
She surely does love the Lord, and everyone will miss

her when she goes home to the many mansions."[5]

On the evening of his twenty-fifth birthday, January 17, 1933, John reflected in his journal: "Today one quarter of a century of my life comes to an end. Tonight I have been much mindful of many failures and many opportunities missed. But I do thank God for those countless blessings all along the way, and look for His leading in the future. I give myself to Thee, Lord Jesus. Use me as Thy tool for Thy glory. Amen."[6]

Despite the fact that a few inches of snow lay on the ground, the next day the young missionaries helped John celebrate his birthday while playing a game of basketball out on the athletic field. At the close of the game they grabbed John, who had refereed the contest, and rolled him over and over in the snow. That evening at supper they presented him with several "gifts," which were a number of his own belongings that had been sneaked from his room. The dinner ended with a special treat of birthday cake and homemade ice cream.

A short while later both John and Betty experienced separate incidences of God's timely financial provision. For some time John had been thinking about a student he had known at Moody Bible Institute, Harry Owen, who was about to make application to serve with the CIM. John desired to send him ten dollars to help him with his outfit fund but had no idea where he would get the money.

"Imagine my delight today," he wrote his relatives, "to have a letter come from Harry telling that he was just about ready to join the CIM, and in the same mail another letter from another man at school, enclosing a *ten-dollar bill*. The Lord knew all about that wish of mine, and in His own wonderful and gracious way enabled me to do the thing that was on my heart."[7]

Betty had been contemplating purchasing some wool blankets that could be used on evangelistic trips. But as she was unsure whether she ought to spend money at that time for that purpose, she prayed, "Dear Lord, if You want me to get these blankets now, would You soon send me in about five dollars just for my own use."

She had not received personal money gifts for a long time and, the Christmas season being past, she had no reason to expect any now. The very next morning, however, she received a letter from John, informing her that three of his relatives had sent him cash gifts to forward on to her. He had already transferred the gifts, which totaled ten dollars, to her account in Shanghai.

That winter was proving to be something of a test of patience for Betty. She was eager to be out working with country women, teaching them to read the Bible. But ongoing, serious illness in the Glittenberg household required her to spend most of her time at the mission compound, helping to minister to that family. This she did willingly, though anxiously awaiting the time when she would be free to work with the Chinese people.

In a letter to John's parents she expressed her outlook on her current circumstances: "It seems as though I am not doing very much of anything, not even getting much farther in my studying; but am learning a great deal in the Lord's training school."[8]

Throughout the Glittenbergs' extended period of illness and recuperation, the four female missionaries at Fowyang took turns caring for their patients throughout the day and evening, as well as helping with housekeeping and local ministry bookkeeping. Mr. Glittenberg was busy with station affairs but helped to care for his family as well. He carried out night nurse duties for weeks until exhaustion forced him to accept assistance with those responsibilities.

Eventually Betty was able to start getting out to visit in homes and to distribute tracts. A tract she gave away the very first time she went out visiting was providentially directed to a woman who lived in another section of the city. She read it and was converted. Later Betty was able to visit her in her home and was delighted to see how happy the woman was in her newfound faith and what an influential testimony she was bearing to her family members and neighbors.

On another occasion Betty, Katie Dodd, and two Bible women ventured out for a day to hold brief meetings at a nearby village and in the private residence of a fairly well-to-do farmer in the region. The quartet of evangelists taught those who attended the meetings some Bible verses and songs, using scrolls that Betty had prepared for that purpose. The Bible women had the opportunity to teach by explaining the meaning of the verses and choruses.

The farmer's wife, Ch'en Sao Tsi, was ill with an unidentified type of pox. Though her eyes and nose were running and she felt miserable, she insisted on sitting in a far corner of the room so she would not miss anything. Several of her sisters-in-law were there with their children, and a number of poorer people from the neighborhood crowded into the doorway to join in the service.

The family was exceedingly hospitable, serving the visitors a large noon meal, and then insisting that they stay for the remainder of the day. Throughout the entire afternoon, between the singing of songs and the reciting of verses, family members kept bringing a variety of snack foods for their guests to eat.

Several times the ill hostess herself got up to serve them. The missionaries were well aware of the danger of contracting her disease, but they did not want to offend the family. Betty later exclaimed to John how they handled the situation: "Oh boy, did Katie and I ever pray, and then boldly eat!"

The following Sunday Ch'en Sao Tsi made the effort to walk into Fowyang to attend the worship service, having determined that her pox was a less serious variety. Her diligence in attending the services, born out of her hunger for spiritual food, deeply impressed Betty: "She's all broken out with it and can't be feeling any too well yet. She'll probably come in for our Bible study group on Wednesday. Something like that means so much in their lives that they'll come if not on their death beds."[9]

Around that same time the CIM opened a new station in Kuoyang, some distance north of Fowyang. The Glittenbergs were asked to transfer to that location to oversee the work there. Mr. Yang, the resident native evangelist in Yingshan, had become resistant to the prospect of Betty and Katie's moving to his city to take up ministry with women as originally planned. So the Glittenbergs thought it best that the two single women accompany them to Kuoyang where their ministry efforts would be both welcomed and appreciated.

This change of plans caused Betty to suggest in a letter to John that perhaps their wedding date would need to be postponed several months for the good of the new work in Kuoyang. His brief journal entry of February 21 reflects his characteristically good-spirited acceptance of the Lord's providential leading in his life: "Praise God for all of His great tender mercies, even if Betty does say in her letter of today that we might have to wait till spring to marry, depending upon who is appointed to go up to Kuoyang with her."[10]

# *fifteen*

The following month, March 1933, proved to be full of both stretching challenges and exciting developments for John. Early March found him boning for his first major Chinese language exam, a three-part affair that stretched over as many days.

"I'm now on the homeward stretch toward the exam," he wrote to relatives, "doing all the memorizing that has to be done for it. I'm trying to get some thousand or fifteen hundred characters fixed in my head, so that I can recognize them, give their sound, tone, meaning, and romanization. Quite a bit of a job, and makes a fellow very thankful when the weekend comes. Never have I been so thankful for the Lord's day in all my life, nor realized how necessary it is to get a real break, as these days."[1]

Two weeks later he was able to write: "Hurrah! This morning I finished the last of the three language exams. I took one a day for the last three days, the first taking two and a half hours, the second taking one hour and three quarters, and the third taking two hours and a quarter. So I'm very glad to be finished, and praise the Lord indeed for His help of which I have been very conscious."[2]

The very next week he faced two other challenges. On Wednesday he had an oral examination in Chinese, which included reading from selected passages and holding a conversation with the pastor of the local church rather than with one of his own teachers. Saturday he was to lead the morning worship in Chinese, his assigned preaching text being John 5:15–23.

The pressure John felt in preparing to preach in Chinese can be gauged by a series of references in his journal that week. Tuesday: "Only making slight headway for Sat. A.M. Chinese Prayers." Thursday: "Hard at work and finding it difficult to prepare for Chinese Prayers on Saturday." Friday: "Still at work on Morning Prayers."

On Saturday afternoon, however, when he typed his weekly letter to his relatives, he was jubilant:

*Hallelujah! Phew, that's been safely accomplished. I mean the Chinese morning prayers I took this morning. When we first began to study, and read what Hudson Taylor said about men preaching in Chinese six months after beginning to study, we smiled. But here it is just one day more than five months after I began to study, and I've already taken morning prayers. Praise the Lord.*

*It was certainly blessed to realize that I could say a bit and get over some ideas which were apparently understood. Not being able to pray in Chinese yet myself, I asked the Chinese*

*pastor to do so. By the way he went over all the
points of the message in his prayer, it was evident that he had understood, even if he was
repeating it all for the benefit of some others
who may not have understood.*[3]

Dixon Hoste, the CIM's executive director, arrived at the
language school two days later, on Monday, March 27, for
the all-important purpose of interviewing the young missionaries and designating where they would go to begin
active service in China. He arrived in Anking at 3:30 A.M.
and joined the students for breakfast a few hours later.
After morning devotions, which Hoste led, the interviews
began, with each student spending an hour or more alone
with the director.

John's interview took place the middle of Tuesday
afternoon. Hoste had stayed in bed all that day, having
come down with a cold, but carried on a full slate of des-
ignations in his bedroom. The director, a former military
officer, always carried himself with a perfectly erect bearing. That day, however, when John entered the room, he
was propped up in bed with pillows behind him, looking
weary.

Said John afterward: "There wasn't a suggestion of
the army about him, and he seemed much more like a
tired old patriarch, who has wanted for long to lay his
burden down. As he sat there, the first thing that came
into my mind was the picture we get in Genesis of the
Patriarch Jacob leaning upon the top of his staff and
blessing his sons."

John was in the room for only a few minutes when
Hoste began to pray. The saintly man continued on in
prayer for fifteen or twenty minutes, asking the Lord's

blessing on John and Betty, the CIM, the native church, and other missionaries.

"I couldn't help but feeling," commented John, "that this wasn't, as is so often the case with us, just a bowing of the head and asking the Lord to bless our deliberations. When he began to pray, he forgot that I had come up to be designated, and was on his most important work, that of intercession."

After that the missionary statesman went on to give John practical advice on a whole array of subjects. His tone was paternal and humble rather than patronizing. Finally, after a full hour had elapsed, Hoste got around to the designation. John was to go to Suancheng, a city about one hundred miles east and a little north of Anking. There he would undertake further language study while getting a start in ministry work, serving with George and Grace Birch, missionaries from Vancouver, British Columbia. It was intended that eventually John would be sent to Tsingteh, seventy miles south of Suancheng, to help open a new station there.

Referring to the appeal that Hoste had issued in 1929 for two hundred new workers to carry out itinerant evangelism in the dangerous inland regions of China, John stated, "So if I'm not out with the two hundred, it looks as if it still will be our privilege to open new territory for the Lord."[4]

With the direction received through this designation, John and Betty were able to consider more definitely when they might marry. A few weeks later, the Lord supplied a highly qualified native Christian woman to work with Katie Dodd and the Glittenbergs, making it unessential that Betty be involved in the new ministry which they anticipated beginning in Kuoyang. That being the case, the engaged couple settled on October 25 as their intended wedding date.

Shortly after Hoste's visit, students started leaving the language school for their new places of service. They parted company, having developed a deep brotherly love and respect for each other.

One later testified, "I shall ever thank God for my acquaintance with John. He was the most spiritual fellow in Anking; it was a joy to talk or work with him. He always seemed to be above difficulties and worries, for he turned them over to God. His example encouraged several (I know it did me) to be more diligent in prayer."

Wrote another: "John was the backbone, humanly speaking, of the spiritual life at Anking that winter. He seemed to know Christ more intimately, more practically than the rest of us. When I was discouraged, he helped me to find the joy of the Lord. John's spirituality was radiant and contagious. He seemed to be always in touch with the source of power, even our Lord Himself."[5]

On Monday, April 13, John left Anking and took a steamer downriver to Wuhu. He spent a month there, devoting time to studying the language and assisting the missionaries who resided there in any way he could.

To his family he wrote: "I'm spending some time in study and the rest wandering around town with Mr. Whipple on local secretarial work. I'm getting down into the shops all I can and practicing the language and am finding out how very, very little I know. When these folk talk to me at ordinary speed it sounds as if they're going like express trains. Then, too, I'm finding out how our teachers limited themselves strictly to our present vocabularies in talking to us, while the ordinary stranger on the street doesn't know our vocabulary."[6]

John was transported by boat on Friday, May 12, along the small river that ran from Wuhu to Suancheng. There he was met by George Birch, who later reported the following: "How clearly I remember the day John arrived at Suancheng. I met him at the launch. He was six feet two, every inch a man. His hearty grip and bright smile clinched our friendship at once. As we proceeded in the sampan [a small boat used in shallow water] the conversation soon turned to the things of God, for John lived with God and loved to talk of the things that were filling his heart."[7]

Suancheng was an old established work. The CIM had an attractive large compound there that included a church, some school buildings, two houses for missionaries, as well as housing for several native Christians who lived on the premises. There was a vibrant children's ministry underway at the mission. Children's classes were held three times during the week, and on Sunday evenings another service, largely dedicated to singing, was attended by over one hundred youngsters. It was planned that John would work with a young Chinese Christian, Mr. Ho, in overseeing these children's ministries.

"It would be hard enough to hold the attention of such a rowdy lot of youngsters at home with a knowledge of my own language," John reminded his family members. "But if I am to have anything to do with these little folk, it's not going to be any easier. So do pray for that."[8]

He enjoyed meeting the committed Christians who lived in Suancheng and neighboring towns. A tailor in Suancheng, Mr. Song, always closed his shop on Sundays and paid his five assistants a full day's wage to attend church with him. His competitors viewed such a practice as financially ludicrous, but Mr. Song believed otherwise, and the Lord prospered his business.

Mr. Pao, a silversmith from the nearby town of Tsung-chiup'u, similarly maintained a strong work-related testimony. Some time earlier, George Birch had showed Pao the Bible's teaching on making Sunday a day of worship and rest rather than of work. At first the native believer balked at the thought of closing his business one day a week, as he was seven hundred dollars in debt. After he was out of debt, he reasoned, he would close his shop on Sundays.

Birch, however, shared several Scripture promises of how the Lord blesses those who walk in faith and obedience before Him. Taking God at His word, Pao made the further step of commitment by devoting all of Sunday to worship. For this faithfulness he was repeatedly and publicly reviled by a fellow silversmith whose place of business was across the street from his own.

But God blessed the obedient believer. Gold came into demand and, by keeping in touch with the outside world, Pao made out better than his competitor in the buying and selling of gold and was soon able to pay off his entire debt.

Then a disastrous fire ravaged the street, consuming all the shops across the way from Pao's, including that of his critical rival. On Pao's side of the street the fire advanced to the edge of his property, slightly damaging the upper part of his shop. Suddenly the wind changed, and the young Christian's property was spared. He was left with no doubt that his heavenly Father was indeed watching out for him.

# *sixteen*

After John had been in Suancheng for less than a week, he and George Birch left on a ten-day itineration of the towns and villages between there and Kwangteh, a city sixty miles to the east. They set out on foot along the newly constructed automobile road the morning of Wednesday, May 17, 1933. Along the way they had numerous opportunities to pass out Gospel tracts and share a word of testimony.

They covered a distance of twenty miles that first day out. Near the end of the day it began to rain, turning the dirt surface of the road, which had not yet been opened to bus traffic, into mud. After walking through mud the last couple of miles, they were glad to stop at an inn for the night where they could get washed off and have a hot meal.

"At every inn at which we stopped for tea, or for meals, or to sleep," John reported, "there would always be people interested in the foreigners. We had many opportunities to distribute tracts and sell Gospels. At almost every place, too, Mr. Birch had an opportunity to preach, often hanging up hymn sheets or a picture scroll. On the trip, several thousands had the Gospel given to them by lip and by the printed page. Many said they had not heard the Gospel story before."[1]

The missionaries got off to bed early that first night. Unlike the inns in northern China where all guests slept in their clothes on one large community bed, the inns in that part of southern Anhwei Province offered separate sleeping rooms for travelers. The thin walls, however, consisted of nothing more than bamboo matting covered with newspapers.

John and George were kept awake late listening to the proprietor's family loudly discuss various matters, including their foreign guests. Rats rustled through the straw that covered the boards on which they slept. Fleas in the straw compounded the discomfort of the night.

On Thursday they again walked twenty miles. Special prayer was offered about the place they were to spend the night, as the last time George Birch had been there he and the native workers who accompanied him had had a very unfriendly reception. That evening, however, many genuinely interested people gathered about the two missionaries. Birch preached to an attentive audience for an hour. John gathered a group of boys and asked one of the older ones to read a portion of Scripture, then gave a short explanation of the passage with his limited Chinese vocabulary.

There was a big thunderstorm overnight so that by the next morning the new road was very muddy. They forded a river to get out of town as the bridge had not yet been built. For three or four miles they labored along the road, their shoes and rubbers picking up a couple of pounds of mud at every step. Stopping, they replaced their heavy muddy shoes with two pairs of socks and straw sandals. The sandals picked up no mud, though sandals and socks were quickly soaked through with muddy water. It rained most of the day, but they were able to traverse the final twenty miles to Kwangteh by evening.

John wrote of their arrival: "There was simply a downpour just about then. The townspeople were treated to the sight of two foreigners—wearing straw sandals, trousers rolled up, one with a sun helmet, and both with umbrellas—'doing the street' in the pouring rain, as we gave out tracts in the shops while waiting for our meal to be prepared. It was good to get to Kwangteh and a hot bath after all that mud."[2]

Saturday, Sunday, and Monday were spent ministering to the small group of Christians who lived in Kwangteh. Daytime meetings were held with the believers, and evening evangelistic sessions for the general public were conducted in the street chapel. On Tuesday they undertook an exhausting trek of nearly thirty miles to the town of Iao Ts'uen up in the mountains. The next morning they had only a short walk over a mountain pass to U Ts'uen, a very poor community but the home of one wealthy individual who owned a considerable amount of farmland and several houses in that area. He leased both the land and the houses at exorbitant prices and further took advantage of his fellow townsmen by lending money at an interest rate that bordered on usury.

To make matters worse, in the previous year the community had been plundered by bandits who carried off not only what little money the people of U Ts'uen had, but also their bedding and other meager furnishings. One old man told the two missionaries how the bandits had hung him up and pulled out the hairs of his long beard one at a time in order to get him to divulge where his money was hidden. The rogues escaped the area with their plunder by pretending to be poor country people who were themselves fleeing from bandits.

There had once been many professing Christians in that region, but nearly all of them turned away from the faith when it did not bring them economic prosperity. Only three believers remained true to their Christian profession and continued to carry out an active witness in the region.

One of those faithful Christians was an older man named Kuang Teh Fuh. Thursday morning he took the missionaries to a village five miles from U Ts'uen. "It was beautiful country," John reported, "with its wooded mountains, stony crags, and a patchwork of rice fields in the valleys. I was very glad the old man could only toddle on slowly, for I feasted my soul on the delightful scenery. It was gorgeous."

He also related a special blessing the Lord provided in the meal they were served at that village. Having come down with a bit of a cold and an upset stomach during the course of the journey, John explained:

*For some days we had been unable to get any real green vegetables to eat, and Chinese diet is often inclined to be heavy and a bit greasy. So, rather than take a chance on what this little village had to provide, we took along a tin of Chinese round biscuits obtained in Kwangteh,*

129

*and we planned to get several boiled eggs and
make it a meal.*

*We arrived at the village about noontime,
and hurried around to invite everybody to the
local tea shop to hear the preaching, so as to
get the people before they went back to the fields
for the afternoon. They came, too, and we had a
great time, Mr. Birch preaching as usual, and
when he finished we sold every last Gospel and
gave away many tracts.*

*While we were busy, Old Kuang had ordered
a meal, so that the proprietress was preparing it
while the preaching was going on. It appeared
as though there was nothing for it but to eat it.
Well, the Lord must have touched the heart of
that proprietress, for she did put on some
spread. The rice was well cooked, and there
were eight central bowls—and, what was a wonder, not one of meat. (The Chinese are great on
giving you a lot of pork fat.) Instead there were
five bowls of green vegetables, and just when we
couldn't get green vegetables anywhere around.
She had evidently drawn from her special
reserve store to spread a feast for these unusual
guests. It was a grand meal.*

*"Can God prepare a table in the wilder-
ness?" [Psalm 78:19] GOD CAN!*[3]

They returned home to Suancheng on Saturday. After
walking seventeen miles in the morning, they hired
sedan chairs to carry them the final ten miles through the
pouring rain.

George Birch afterward testified of John: "On our first

itineration together we had to walk all one day in the rain and mud, but John's ardor was in no way dampened. That trip, and all our trips together, were a blessing to me, for John's mind was a mine of wealth in the knowledge of God. He truly was mighty in the Scriptures, full of zeal to make Christ known, and full of love to the lost souls around him.

"John was very quick to see the hand of God in everything. He often said, 'My heavenly Father knows.' And once when speaking of difficulties to face, he quoted the Lord's words, 'For this cause came I unto this hour.' "[4]

John's positive perspective on the itineration was reflected in the closing remark he made at the end of a letter to his family: "This is the type of work I hope to be doing for the years to come—getting out into the country, helping to build up the few struggling saints here and there, and preaching to the heathen in the towns and villages about, and in every tea shop along the road."[5] The letter was cheerfully signed, as most of his from China were, "Yours in His Happy Service, John."[5]

Betty, too, was encouraged in her ministry endeavors at Fowyang at that same time. A young seminary-trained native Christian named Miss P'eng had come to work with Katie Dodd and her. It had been decided that Miss P'eng would accompany Katie when she moved to Kuoyang to minister to women there.

One noon Betty, Katie, and Miss P'eng went to have lunch in the home of one of the elected church officers. Though the church leader had been a Christian for some time, he so revered his deceased mother that he had never taken down the idolatrous ancestral tablet that occupied a prominent position of honor in the home— hung on the wall among Bible mottos and pictures.

"It was Miss P'eng," reported Betty, "who called his attention, clearly and yet very reasonably and kindly, to the inconsistency."

As a result, the man burned the ancestral tablet. As he did so, with his family gathered around, his young daughter began to cry. "Oh, you're burning up Grandmother!" she cried.

"No, my precious little one," the father reassured the youngster. "We are not hurting Grandmother. She is already dead and gone. We will not forget her and will continue to honor her. But neither she nor any of our ancestors should be worshiped. We worship only the one true God."

# *seventeen*

The last week of June, George and Grace Birch left Suancheng for two months of much-needed rest at a primitive mountain resort. Chinese missionaries, worn down after months of ceaseless, sacrificial labor, commonly spent a few weeks during the hottest part of the summer at a cooler seaside or mountain retreat for personal restoration.

John had been invited to join the Scotts at their seaside retreat that summer but declined. New missionaries normally did not take an extended vacation during their first year of service, and he desired to stay focused on his study of Chinese to gain a better command of the language as quickly as possible.

He certainly had the opportunity that summer. After only eight months in China he was left as the only missionary on the CIM's Suancheng premises for a period of nine weeks. As he carried out the children's work, participated in Chinese worship and prayer services, inter-acted daily with the natives who lived on the compound, and took advantage of numerous other ministry opportu-nities, he had occasion to use the language constantly.

"Well, I'm all alone now—a regular bachelor," he wrote to his family on July 1. "But it's not half as bad as it sounds. A good letter from a friend back home did a lot to make me remember my great privilege the one day I almost began to get a bit tinged with blueing."

"What I've been enjoying most," he added later in that same letter, "has just been to get out, distribute a few tracts, and get a chance to talk to people. Last night I stopped in two shops where men asked me to sit down for awhile. I had a good little chance to speak to them about the Gospel, except for the fact that my vocabulary is still so awfully limited."[1]

Nine days later he wrote these words to relatives: "Many thanks are certainly due to you folk for your faith-fulness in writing. Hardly a U.S. mail goes by without a letter from home. You can imagine how I do look for mail these days. However, I'm not lonely, and the Lord has given me great peace and joy."[2]

But it was inevitable that John experience some sense of isolation that summer. On August 4 he recorded privately in his journal, "Thank God for His own great comfort when that call—'Foreigner!'—is constantly heard on the street. It does make one feel like he is in a strange land."[3]

Attendance at the children's meetings actually de-clined the first couple of weeks John led them. One Thurs-day meeting began with only three youngsters present and ended with a mere ten. He prayed and persevered through the discouraging slump, however, and attendance re-bounded to sixty by the following Saturday.

John began those meetings by leading the children in singing hymns and Gospel choruses. Then he gave out a poetical essay for children that shared the Gospel story, having the children repeat it back to him a line at a time. As his facility in the language grew, he was able to start telling short Bible stories as well.

He wrote to relatives in mid-August: "One's heart can be gladdened by hearing the children going down the street singing away at the top of their lungs, 'Yes, Jesus Loves Me.' I have been keeping up the children's meetings three times a week, and have been more than repaid in hearing the children sing their choruses just about all day long. If I cannot give the message to their folk, the children most certainly do in the words of many Scripture choruses."[4]

John also received regular visits from teenaged students. He always had a good Gospel tract handy, which he would give to one of the young people and ask to read for all to hear. Then he would offer a brief further explanation.

"As yet," he wrote in the middle of July, "I can't do what I should like to—give them leading questions that will bring out what they think and believe, and then try to give them something to fit their needs. My vocabulary is still too limited, and I still only understand a fraction of what they say. Many of them, too, are probably more interested in just seeing the foreigner, and they all want to hear the phonograph, and some of them the organ. But they get a little Gospel from me by word of mouth and more in a tract or Gospel booklet."[5]

A month later he was able to report: "I have been much helped in the study of the language and especially in the spoken language, being all alone with the Chinese as I am. I can't say I have a good chum, but I must say that almost every day high school students stop in. I always endeavor to go through a chapter of Scripture with them and explain it."[6]

While the Birches were away, John tended their garden, getting up early to work for an hour each morning "for my exercise and delight at the same time." Not knowing how to store potatoes in that hot climate, a good portion of the seventy-pound crop he harvested in July was lost. He did succeed, however, in canning other vegetables and fruits, as well as in making batches of jam. Periodic notations in his diary recorded some of his progress in that regard:

"August 5—Today finished canning 23 quarts of pears. 10 quarts of tomatoes already canned."

"August 19—These last few days or a week seem largely to have been taken up with making jam."

His journal entry of August 28 reveals that he had a pleasant surprise awaiting the Birches upon their return: "Word from George that he is returning tomorrow. Every jar but one is packed with preserves and jam. Thank the Lord for all His help on all lines."

Early in August John had reason to be concerned for Betty's welfare in Fowyang. News had come that for several days the gates of that city were kept tightly shut as a bandit army laid siege. A group of soldiers went out to drive off the bandits but ended up joining forces with them. Except for a militia of volunteers who kept vigilant watch on the city walls, there was no one left to protect the city. After a week of having its gates firmly closed, Fowyang began to face the danger of a food shortage.

News of the city's peril got out, and the government in Nanking, 180 miles to the east, sent airplanes to bomb the bandit forces. The bandits scattered to neighboring villages and the siege was broken. Great was John's relief when he learned that relative security had once again been restored to Fowyang.

For nearly six months the area right around Suancheng had received little rain, so that by early August the rice crop was in great danger of drying up. Day after day, long processions of people made their way through the streets of town and out to a temple on a distant hill.

The crashing of large brass cymbals announced the approach of each procession. At the head of the train was an idol set upright in a sedan chair that was being carried by two bearers. A large crowd of men followed behind the idol, sometimes shouting out as they moved along. Each man carried a small bamboo stick with a few dried leaves and a banner on the end of it. On the banner was written a prayer, beseeching the idol to send rain. The leaves were intended to show the idol how desperately dry conditions had become.

In humbling themselves before the idol, none of the men wore hats. They shielded their heads from the scorching sun by covering them with a lily leaf or with a wreath of small, leafy branches.

For two weeks the local magistrate, an ardent worshiper of the gods, had commanded that no meat or fish be sold. It was thought that by temporarily becoming vegetarians, the people might be able to appease their gods who must be angry with them.

"Oh, how I have longed to get out and stop them," John wrote of the misled masses, "and tell them to turn their prayers to the One True God, instead of that helpless idol that they even have to carry along. Oh, the sin of the people and the shame of those who worship false gods, and neither thank nor recognize with their prayers the One and Only True and Great God of Heaven and Earth. It gives one an awful feeling of powerlessness not to be able to help them."[7]

If John was not yet able to appeal to the masses, he was progressing in his ability to communicate with individuals. One evening at that same time he went into a Confucian temple and shared a Gospel testimony with four young men. On his way home he spotted a few boys standing beside the city wall, throwing rocks over into the river a short distance away. He joined in their sport for a few minutes, and then began to pass out tracts and share a verbal testimony. Soon a group of ten children and adults were gathered around listening to him.

"Do you really know that your sins are forgiven?" he asked the members of his small audience. "Or how about other people you meet out on the street? Are any of them certain that their sins are forgiven?"

"No" and "Of course not" were the responses.

"I know that my sins are forgiven," John stated definitely. "I don't just *hope* they're forgiven. I *know* they are."

Seeing the surprise on the people's faces, he continued: "I know that, not because I haven't any sins, but because Christ died for my sins. Jesus, the sinless Son of God, died on the cross to pay the penalty for my sins so that I could be forgiven.

"He did the same for you also. You, too, can be forgiven by trusting in Jesus as your Savior from sin. That's what these pamphlets talk about. I hope you'll read them carefully and believe what they say."

Just before the Birches returned, John was asked to lead worship and preach at the Sunday service of Suancheng's large Chinese congregation. On Monday, August 28, the day after the challenging assignment had

been successfully carried out, he wrote to his relatives
back home:

> *Pastor Li asked me on Tuesday if I would lead*
> *Sunday morning service. This is quite a church*
> *here, with two pastors and others who can*
> *preach beside, so I was very hesitant to say yes,*
> *realized my lack of language. But he insisted,*
> *and since I always have a hard time refusing*
> *opportunities to preach the Gospel, I consented.*
>
> *If I ever had any doubt as to my ability to*
> *express myself in Chinese, it certainly was*
> *strengthened soon enough. That very afternoon in*
> *the children's meeting I had about the worst time*
> *I ever had. Some of the children began to mimic*
> *me. That's bad enough when they do it in your*
> *own language for some peculiarity. But when*
> *they do it in another language, and you can't see*
> *what you're saying wrong, it's different.*
>
> *Then all through the week I seemed to get*
> *into difficult situations where my language was*
> *insufficient. However, on Sunday the Lord did*
> *help very blessedly.*[8]

# *eighteen*

After the Birches returned to Suancheng, John was able to devote more time to his language study. He was pressing hard, desiring to complete the second major language exam the CIM required of its new missionaries before he left in the middle of October for his wedding in Tsinan. In a letter dated September 9, he revealed the following:

"This week I've just been keeping my nose right down to that language grindstone, for I'm working hard trying to finish Section II before I go to Tsinan. If I don't finish it by then, it will mean a month or more gathering up the threads again after the wedding trip.

"With school started, the students aren't coming every day anymore, although today seven of them came again. Praise the Lord. Pray much for these boys. They are very intelligent, and today they asked about joining church. Although how much real heart interest this

140

betokens, only the Lord knows."

Earlier that week John found himself discussing the weather with three Chinese friends, an incident he related in the same letter. "This has been one of the hottest summers we have had in a long time," commented one native.

"The heat has been terrible," agreed another.

"And to think," John commented, "how the Lord has protected me all through it with health and a good measure of comfort. I've been well able to sleep and to study, while even a lot of the Chinese during the hot weather say they can't do anything. So praise the Lord indeed."[1]

But John was pushing himself in his studies, and soon he found himself going through a spiritually dry period. Early in September he reflected in his diary: "Somehow or other I feel rather barren spiritually. Oh, Lord, make Thy servant fit for Thy use."

Three days later he added, "I feel much the need of a real refreshing from the presence of God. For some days have been feeling cold and dead. Oh, that God would make me more usable."[2]

As John forged ahead in his language studies, Betty left Fowyang for her parents' home in Tsinan. Bandits were still a threat in the area but, trusting God for protection, she set out by river boat. As she was leaving Fowyang for good, she took with her all her possessions, which included no furniture but bedding, clothing, books, dishes, and other personal items. Her only companion was a small Chinese boy whom she was helping transport safely to school.

It rained throughout those first two days of river travel. She and her relatives reflected afterward that the rain may well have been sent as a divine protection. The Chinese had a strong aversion to being out in the rain, and even bandits would be far less likely to move about under those wet conditions.

She arrived at the railroad station at Pengpu, a few hours north of Nanking, at 11 P.M. An express train was leaving at midnight, but she needed to have her bags checked, and the inspector worked only during the daytime. Fortunately, there was a Presbyterian outstation nearby where she and her young companion could spend the night. After getting her goods to shore by rowboat in the rain, she was able to hire coolies to transport them to the mission house. They found the home clean and comfortable, and a Chinese watchman treated them solicitously.

The next day she was detained further as customs officials had become suspicious that some of her boxes might contain guns or explosives. She was finally able to have the containers opened so their contents could be proven harmless. This done, she was able to catch the next train to Tsinan. Fifteen hours later, she was relieved to arrive at her parents' home.

John was highly encouraged through an itineration that he and George Birch undertook the last weekend in September. They set out for a CIM outstation in Huang Tu, about fourteen miles from Suancheng. Stopping at a tea shop along the way to distribute tracts, John was overjoyed to discover that he could both understand what people were saying and be understood by them.

"I came away full of thankfulness to God," he rejoiced afterward, "as it dawned on me so suddenly that at last the Lord had opened my mouth at least a little bit. It was great to be able to give the way of salvation and sometimes to understand their comments and questions, too."[3]

Along the way they passed a small temple that was

dedicated to the weasel, an animal many of the Chinese venerated. All around the temple were wooden boards, placed there by those who had come to pray at the shrine. On each board was engraved the Chinese character that meant efficacious, signifying something effective and powerful.

On one side of the temple was a long pole from which individuals had suspended small stuffed cloth imitations of arms, legs, hands, eyes, and other body parts. These were left to remind the weasel idol which limb or organ the petitioner desired to have restored.

In Huang Tu the missionaries were the guests of Mr. P'en, a respected physician. Friday evening they stayed up late talking about spiritual matters with the towns-people who had crowded into Mr. P'en's home. The next day, accompanied by Mr. P'en, they made their way down the street in Huang Tu, stopping in nearly every shop along the way and having many good spiritual dis-cussions. At the edge of town, under a tree, they gathered the curious children who had been following them, taught them a chorus, and had a Bible lesson with them.

Despite the rather run-down condition of the outsta-tion's chapel building, the Sunday morning church ser-vice was well attended. That afternoon the missionaries started on the return journey to Suancheng. After walk-ing several miles, they stopped to spend the night at the large farmhouse of a clan. There a set of aging parents lived under one roof with several adult sons and their families. The sons, who all shared the same surname, were distinguished by number, being called First Son, Second Son, and so on. Honorable Son Number Five was the family schoolteacher. That evening the whole clan and some neighbors gathered in the room that had

143

been set aside for the school in order to listen to the missionaries. John was able to share a brief Gospel message.

It rained nearly all night. The next morning the missionaries once again donned straw sandals to aid them in walking the several remaining miles along muddy roads back to Suancheng. John returned feeling refreshed and encouraged. He had enjoyed immensely the opportunities to minister, and the brief itineration had provided him with a timely break from his intensive Chinese studies. He was also enormously encouraged that he was making definite progress in the language.

The first two weeks of October John worked furiously at his studies in order to take the second major language exam before leaving for Tsinan. "Was much helped of the Lord," he recorded in his diary on October 11, "in learning some 280 characters in the writing lessons very quickly."[4]

The next two days, a Thursday and Friday, he had an oral exam and a three-part written exam that took over eight hours to complete. Friday evening he moved his belongings out of the home where he had been staying with the Birches and into the neighboring house he and Betty would share after returning from their honeymoon. He started to pack for his trip late that night but was so exhausted that he went to bed with the task unfinished.

Saturday morning he was up early to finish packing in time to catch the launch from Suancheng to Wuhu. Along the way he had several good opportunities to share a Christian witness. The boat's proprietor was so pleased with the gift of a Chinese New Testament John gave to him that he insisted on providing the missionary with a free meal.

"These boat trips (I've had three of them) have all seemed to mark some progress in the language," John told his relatives in a brief letter which he wrote to them while staying in Wuhu for one day. "The first trip, up to Anking, found me without any understanding of the language. The next one, down to Suancheng six months later, was more interesting, for I could understand a little bit, but still could scarcely say anything. But this one was thoroughly enjoyable, for I could give the Gospel to my cabin mate and to the visitors who came in to see the foreigner."

Giving expression to the gratitude welling up in his heart at that moment, he wrote further: "I think I shall have to take a couple of days off just to praise the Lord and to thank Him, the which also I should like to do for the following reasons:

1. That I'm saved and in the Lord's service.

2. For excellent health despite the hottest summer here in years and a change in climate, too.

3. Great advance in the language.

4. Maybe this ought to be #2. That, God willing, I shall soon be returning with 'my wife.' I like that phrase, too."[5]

# nineteen

John took advantage of other opportunities to share his faith en route to Tsinan. In Wuhu on Sunday he met two British naval officers to whom he gave English New Testaments. The next day he traveled by bus to Nanking. Although he had intended to do some shopping, after meeting an American aviator named Hazzard, he spent all day with him, visiting the tombs of the Ming Dynasty.

Afterward he reported, "Had a good chance to talk to him and to the table boy who waited on me. I do pray that the Lord will bless my testimony."[1]

Monday and Tuesday nights he tried to get some sleep while traveling by train first to Tsenghsien, then to Tsinan. Arriving in Tsinan early in the morning on Wednesday, October 18, he made his way to the Scotts' home. There he met Betty, exactly one year to the day since they had last seen each other when they parted in Shanghai.

The couple appreciated having two days together by themselves before members of the wedding party started arriving. Then they joyously welcomed Betty's maid of honor, Marguerite Luce, her two bridesmaids, Katie Dodd and Nancy Rodgers, and John's groomsman, Percy Bromley.

Marguerite, who had been Betty's roommate and closest friend at Wilson College, was now a missionary nurse serving at the Presbyterian hospital in Chefoo, China. Katie and Nancy had become Betty's beloved coworkers while they labored together in Fowyang. John had come to love and respect Percy during their time together at language school in Anking. Percy had excelled all his fellow students in the learning of Chinese and was nicknamed "Crudens" (after the Bible concordance bearing that same name) by some of his classmates because of his extensive knowledge of Scripture.

On Sunday they attended the Tsinan Chinese Church service in the morning. That evening John was asked to preach at the English service in the Presbyterians' University Chapel. Donning a robe for the occasion, he spoke on Psalm 24.

The weather on John and Betty's wedding day, Wednesday, October 25, 1933, was perfect. There was not a cloud in the sky all day and no wind to stir up dust. The temperature was warmer than it had been for several days. The wedding party and family members were all deeply thankful for these blessings as they had hoped to have an outside ceremony in order to accommodate more guests.

The compound's tennis court on the east side of the Scotts' house was converted into an open-air chapel. Long benches with backs were carried over from the compound church and arranged in a semicircle with a wide aisle down the middle. The court was lined with trees and

147

shrubs on three sides. On its south side was a low wall covered with a solid mass of ivy, the leaves of which were turning red and gold. As the assembled guests looked out over that wall they saw a series of high hills in the distance. The south end of the court, where the wedding party stood during the ceremony, was further decorated with palms, ferns, and flowering plants. Rugs covered the cement floor and a red carpet was laid down the center aisle.

About two hundred guests had been invited to the wedding: eighty foreigners, sixty Chinese leaders, and sixty older students whom the Scotts taught in Tsinan. Charles Scott had arranged to have various classical music selections playing on the phonograph as the guests arrived and were seated. Promptly at 4:00 in the afternoon the traditional "Wedding March" from Wagner's *Lohengrin* was struck up on the piano in the Scotts' living room, being easily heard through the open windows.

John and Percy, led by the Rev. Reuben A. Torrey Jr., took their places up front. Torrey was the son of the world-renowned American evangelist Dr. R. A. Torrey. His ministerial robes and dignified air added to the solemnity and reverence of the ceremony.

The bridesmaids and maid of honor, wearing lavender silk dresses and carrying bouquets of yellow chrysanthemums and asparagus ferns tied with yellow ribbons, made their way one at a time down the center aisle. Finally came Betty, escorted by her father. Her wedding gown was made of white silk crepe and had wide sleeves and a long circular skirt. Brussels lace lined the neck of her gown and the front of her veil.

On her lips was a sweet, happy smile as she looked steadily upon John's face. This was in contrast to many Chinese weddings, even among Christians, where the bride never even glanced up into the face of the bride-groom but kept her head bowed as if in sorrow or trepidation. That was considered a sign of respect for the husband.

"The wedding went off beautifully," John wrote to family members, "or at least so everybody said. About the only thing I know was that Betty looked very, very beautiful as she came down the aisle at her father's side. Then I led her to the minister and the words of that beautiful marriage ceremony began."[2]

Unknown to John at the time, his parents back in Paterson, New Jersey, had gotten out of bed at 2:30 A.M. in order to be in prayer throughout the exact hour of the wedding. They prayed for the Lord's blessing on John and Betty as they began their new life together and asked that the ceremony might go well and bring great glory to God.

The Scotts reported of the wedding to their acquaintances back home: "Everyone seemed to feel a reverence and sacred joy as they witnessed the uniting in holy wedlock of two such devoted, consecrated young lives. Many of the guests, Chinese and foreign, spoke later of the helpfulness of the service to them."[3]

At the conclusion of the ceremony, the bridal party, joined by Betty's parents, turned around where they were standing and greeted the guests, who readily stepped forward to offer their congratulations. Tables of refreshments had been placed at the north end of the tennis courts. The guests were served wedding cake, cookies, tea, and fruit punch.

Early that evening, after the guests had departed, the bridal party enjoyed a wedding supper together. Then they shared a time of devotions in which they sang, read a portion of Scripture, reflected on God's manifold blessings, and prayed. At about nine thirty John and Betty left the

Scotts' home and went to spend the night at Stein's Hotel. The next day they left on the noon train for Tsingtao, Betty's childhood home. They were to spend two weeks there, staying in the house her parents had built and planned to live in after their retirement.

John's letters home during their two-week honeymoon overflowed with exuberant joy and thanksgiving: "October 27—This letter finds *us* at Tsingtao—a young married couple. Oh, the Lord has been so good in all the arrangements that we have just been praising Him all along the way. We're just having a most blessed time together. I've such a lot of things to tell you that I'm going to see if I can lay my hands on some typewriter around here before the Lord's blessings pile up so high that I shall forget a good many of them. Truly our God seems to go way out of His way to make His children happy."[4]

In his letter of October 31 he described their honeymoon setting and activities: "Tsingtao is built on a big peninsula, or series of them, with many high mountains and lots of woods. The place in which we stay is on the side of a high hill overlooking the beach, the far peninsula, and the sea beyond. It's just gorgeous, and Betty and I are daily enjoying our walks around the hills. The trees are just turning and the air has that delightful autumn tang to it.

"We've been out to meals a few times to some old friends of the Scotts here in Tsingtao. But most of the time we are out walking, or home reading, and just simply enjoying ourselves. Incidentally, I guess this is the first real vacation I've had with nothing to do for years and years."[5]

A friend of Betty's father took them up to his cottage in the mountains about two hours from Tsingtao so the couple could enjoy a night alone there. Mighty rock peaks towered all around and the trees were displaying their autumn colors. The next morning John and Betty walked up a valley toward a scenic waterfall that was surrounded by crystal-clear pools and large rocks. Throughout the entire walk they saw only two other people. In that isolated setting they felt free to give full vent to the joy that welled up within them by merrily singing, whistling, and even yodeling together.

One day they were discussing a missionary acquaintance who was ministering all on his own in an isolated location in China. Reflecting the newlywed bliss in her own heart, Betty queried, "John, dear, don't you wish all our single friends would get married?" He readily concurred.

While in Tsingtao John and Betty had the joy of learning of the surprising spiritual transformation of a foreign businessman there. Betty's first acquaintance with the man came during her voyage to China as a new missionary when he rebuked her and her friends for holding Sunday school sessions with the children aboard the ship. Since then, however, he had been thoroughly converted and was now seeking to win others to Christ.

On Wednesday, November 8, they boarded a ship for Shanghai. Betty's parents, who were paying all honeymoon expenses as their wedding gift to the young couple, insisted that they sail first class. John's perpetual missionary perspective is seen in his journal entry the next day: "Beautiful day, sunshiny and calm. The only fly in the ointment was that I didn't speak to anyone aboard the ship about his soul."[6]

They spent several busy days in Shanghai, shopping for necessary supplies to take with them to Suancheng, visiting a dentist, having a wedding portrait taken by a professional photographer, attending church services and prayer meetings, as well as enjoying meals or tea with a number of missionary acquaintances. Thursday and Friday, November 16 and 17, they traveled up the Yangtze by steamer to Wuhu.

Again John was faithful to share his faith along the way, as he recorded in his diary afterward: "Had quite a talk with the Purser, a Mr. Ellis, a man entirely satisfied with his own good character."[7]

The following Monday the young missionary couple set out for Suancheng by launch. Two or three times along the way the craft ran aground on a sandbar and needed to maneuver its way slowly through shallow water. The launch traveled only to within five miles of Suancheng. John and Betty were relieved to find George Birch and Song the tailor waiting for them with a pair of rowboats.

After two hours of rowing they arrived at their destination. George instructed the weary travelers to go on ahead while he and Song arranged to have their belongings transported to the mission compound. The city gates had already been closed for the night but were opened to admit first John and Betty, then George, Song, and the coolies who were assisting them with the luggage.

It was well after midnight by the time John and Betty settled into bed that night. They were extremely happy finally to be in the house that would serve as their first home.

# twenty

John and Betty spent their first few days in Suancheng unpacking their belongings and getting their new home settled to their satisfaction. They also lost no time in getting involved in ministry opportunities at their station and in the region.

The evening after they arrived they attended the mission's weeknight Bible class. "Had a big attendance," John revealed afterward, "which was accounted for in part by the curiosity as to what that new bride looked like."[1]

The following Sunday, November 26, John accompanied two native evangelists to the local jail where they held a service for about forty men. Most of the prisoners looked very poor and two of them had irons on their feet. One of the Chinese evangelists, a former opium smoker who had been delivered from his addiction through his conversion to Christ, shared his testimony. John proclaimed the Gospel to the men, using John 3:16 as his text.

Both John and Betty helped in the leading of the children's meetings held during the week and on Sunday evenings. A number of girl students began dropping by to visit with Betty, and soon she was leading them in a Bible study.

On the first day of December 1933, the young missionary couple began meeting with a native teacher to aid them in making further progress in learning the Chinese language. They often devoted the morning hours to language study, John sitting at one end and Betty at the other of a small table that had been set up in the living room for that purpose.

"I must say that John has gotten the language *wonderfully* in a year, both written and spoken," Betty wrote to his parents about that time. "Everybody remarks on it. He has gotten idiom and tones especially well, and understands a great deal of what is being said."

With the weather turning cold, John and Betty hired tailors to make fur-lined clothes for them. "You ought to see John in his Chinese garments!" Betty commented in that same correspondence. "He looks taller than usual. And watch him gather his arms up under the skirts in back when he's going down stairs, for all the world like an old Chinese gentleman!"[2]

On December 8 George Birch and John traveled, mainly by rowboat, to Ma Shan P'u, a village twenty miles from Suancheng where there was a CIM outstation. There they devoted the morning to personal study and prayer and the afternoon and evening to visiting the people and having meetings.

"George Birch evolved that plan," John explained to his relatives in a letter, "and I must say I like it better than rushing out in the A.M. without a good time for prayer and Bible study. One does sometimes get to feeling like a dry well, and we need to drink lots from the wells of God if we are to have water for others."

Friday and Saturday evenings the little chapel in Ma Shan P'u was crowded with children eager to learn and sing the choruses the missionaries taught them. After the chapel services the children followed the evangelists into the inn where they wanted to stay and sing songs rather than return to their own homes.

They rowed back to Suancheng on Monday, just in time to participate in an open-air meeting that evening. John commented: "We had a good street chapel meeting in the evening, in which the Lord most certainly helped me. It is beginning to be enjoyable to speak a bit of Chinese."[3]

About a week later John and Betty traveled, along with Mr. Song, the tailor, to minister at the outstation in Tsungchiup'u, the hometown of Mr. Pao, the silversmith. On Saturday the four evangelists went around distributing tracts and talking with people in their homes. That evening they had a crowded meeting in the street chapel next to Pao's place of business. Sunday proved an extremely busy and blessed day. In the morning they had a worship service, after which the Lord's Supper was observed. That afternoon they held a service in the chapel, and then went out to have two open-air meetings. A large, attentive audience gathered in the chapel again that evening.

The missionary band took its time returning home to Suancheng the next day. The distance of ten miles was covered in a leisurely six hours, providing plenty of opportunity to stop and share a Gospel witness to groups of people encountered along the way. They had an impromptu outdoor meeting in the village where they stopped for lunch. "We finally arrived at Suancheng,"

John shared, "with every tract given out and every Gospel sold, and with a big blessing in our own souls."[4]

In January of 1934, John, Betty, and Miss Kiang, a gifted native Bible teacher who ministered in and around Suancheng, were to travel to Kwangteh to hold meetings with the church members and inquirers there. As the previously arranged date approached, however, the Christians in Kwangteh wrote requesting that the meetings be postponed. Their church building was not yet completed and the present time did not seem convenient to host a series of meetings.

Miss Kiang had already left Suancheng, being at a set of meetings in another town. Not knowing if a letter informing her of the change in plans would reach her in time, John set out for the place where he and Betty had agreed to meet Miss Kiang along the way to Kwangteh. After leaving word there for Miss Kiang, he continued on to Kwangteh, as by then it was Saturday afternoon and he did not have time to walk the nearly twenty miles back to Suancheng.

The Kwangteh Christians received him warmly and agreed to hold three days of meetings with him since providential circumstances had brought him there. The band of faithful believers met three times a day for prayer and Bible study.

After two days of heavy snowfall it began to look like John might need to remain in Kwangteh for a week or longer until the roads became passable again. To John, that prospect was not the most inviting: Further ministry opportunities in Kwangteh were limited, and his accommodations in a drafty, unfinished room in the new chapel left much to be desired.

Early Thursday evening he was astonished to learn

that an English-speaking foreign couple had arrived in town in a car. Having inquired if there were any other foreigners in town who might be of assistance to them, the couple was led to John.

After introducing himself, the man explained: "I'm an engineer helping to build bridges for the railroad line which is being put through this area. My wife and I are trying to make our way to Suancheng where we intend to make our home, and I'll work out from there. When we arrived at Wuhu we discovered there isn't a road from there to Suancheng. So we've circled back around Nanking and Hangchow, completely out of our way, to get on this new road, which we're told will lead us to Suancheng. We had hoped to make it there yet tonight, but arrived here just too late to press on."

"Suancheng is where I live," John revealed. "My wife and I are missionaries there. I had some church meetings here earlier in the week, but have been unable to return home due to the snow."

"Do you think you could help us find a place to get supper and an inn where we can spend the night?" the engineer asked.

"Surely," John responded.

The traveler, looking relieved, offered, "In exchange for your trouble, we would be glad to take you to Suancheng in the morning."

John and the Kwangteh believers were jubilant over this obvious instance of God's providential provision for one of His servants. Remarked John, "Surely the Lord does watch over His own, even if He makes a couple of unbelievers travel hundreds of extra miles through all kinds of trouble just to get to him in the nick of time."

At the time of the Chinese New Year, in February of

157

1934, John and Betty made a longer trip to the extreme southern region of Anhwei Province where they were to take up residence later in the year when another missionary couple, Mr. and Mrs. Sam Warren, left on furlough. During the twenty-four-day itineration, they traveled some two hundred miles on foot and another thirty-five miles by boat.

On the third day of the journey they entered the mountainous terrain of southern Anhwei where they were met by Mr. Warren. He escorted them to the home of the Li family in the town of Kuan In Ch'iao. Both evenings they were there a good number of people packed into the family's guest room and listened attentively to the Gospel message.

One of the Chinese believers there told the missionaries, "Last year I was beaten for refusing to carry an idol in the rain processions. I prayed to the true God and was beaten for my stand."

Saturday morning they went on to another town, Miaosheo. There they stayed in the home of a widow, Mrs. Wang, the first individual in that entire region to have become a Christian.

Years earlier a missionary couple, Mr. and Mrs. Gibb, were passing through the area and stopped to spend the night at Miaosheo. Before they had even found a place to stay, Mr. Gibb began to preach. Mrs. Wang and her husband heard the message and immediately believed. They invited the missionaries into their home for the night.

When asked if she believed this new doctrine, Mrs. Wang responded, "I do not see how one could do anything but believe when told of such wonderful love."

At the time of their conversion, the nearest Christian

church was twenty miles away in Chiki. Twice a month, even during the busy rice-planting season, Mr. Wang would go there to attend services. He left Miaosheo on Saturday, stayed in Chiki all Sunday, and returned home on Monday.

John and Betty next traveled twelve miles across the mountains to Tsingteh where they spent a week with the Warrens. Tsingteh had once been a wealthy city, a favorite residence of noble families who attended the emperor. But the brutal T'ai-ping Rebellion some seventy years earlier had left much of Tsingteh in ruins. Though extensive portions of the city had never been rebuilt, many of Tsingteh's large old homes still stood and were occupied.

Betty described the city and the CIM residence there in a letter: "The people live in more comparative comfort, eat better food, and are probably more self-satisfied. Many live in old houses full of spacious halls, wonderful carved wooden beams and shutters. Even in the inns coming down we rarely encountered a single flea or allied pest—a thing unheard of in the north.

"The premises here are thoroughly Chinese, but big and roomy. We really have a fine street chapel at the front, and a comfortable place to live in the rear, made out of one of the old Chinese houses. It used to be an opium den, then a cloth shop in front and a private school behind."[5]

The Warrens had been ministering in Tsingteh for about a year. Prior to that, missionaries had lived there only sporadically and for short periods of time. Only one or two of the townspeople professed to be Christians.

"Ancestor worship with the strong clan systems form our greatest barrier throughout the whole region," John explained to relatives in a letter. "Families have lived here for generations. Idols are very few in these places. Mostly there are great halls with bank upon bank of ancestral tablets rising up toward the ceiling. In Tsingteh alone there are said to be thirteen ancestral halls just for the Lu family.

"For centuries back many of these people have been of the gentry class, with ancestors and relatives as officials at court to supply the means of living. Now they live on the proceeds of the clan property which is divided once a year. Anyone following the Christian doctrines and refusing to join in their ceremonies stands the chance of having his income cut off as well as being deprived the use of the family name. A farmer of the clan may find his fields taken away or his water supply cut off. So it is only the power of God that can work against such powers of coercion."[6]

Leaving Tsingteh on a Monday, John and Betty turned southward and crossed the border into Chekiang Province. That evening they had a good meeting with the believers in Chiki. After that they traveled two days north to the town of Changhwa. Several meetings were held as they spent a few days in that general vicinity. In Changhwa they met Pastor Cheng and his small but faithful congregation of eighteen members.

Some thirty years earlier Pastor Cheng's father, then a schoolteacher, bought a copy of the Gospels and Acts from a colporteur who passed through that region. As he read the Scripture books, he became convinced that they taught spiritual truth. When the colporteur visited the area again, Mr. Cheng eagerly asked him, "Is there not more of this story? From my reading I have discovered that I have only part of a larger book."

The bookseller hastened to supply the searching man

with an entire Bible. Later, Mr. Cheng was baptized by Mr. Gibb, the missionary who had led the Wangs to Christ in Miaosheo. Shortly after committing his life to Christ the schoolteacher's eyesight began to fail. "This is happening because you won't worship the idols," his neighbors told him.

When his grandmother died sometime later, the same thing was said. "No," the new convert insisted, "she died of natural causes. She was already sixty years old." At that time in China sixty years was considered a long life span.

Next Cheng's son became violently ill. When the appeals of relatives to the father were unavailing, they went to the son. "May we have your permission to worship and appease the idols in your behalf? Our supplications will do you no good if your unbelief angers the gods."

"No," responded the boy who had also become a firm Christian believer. "We pray to and worship the True God. He will hear our prayers. Praying to idols will do no good."

This son recovered and went on to become the pastor of the church in Changhwa. The Chengs were threatened with the confiscation of their house and fields, but they remained true to the Lord.

From there the missionary couple traveled back over the mountains into Anhwei Province. With Betty's weakened heart, it had been necessary for her to travel in a sedan chair during much of the itineration. The only chair carriers available that day were a cause for some concern. One was a short-winded older man who had been an opium addict for over forty years, while the other was a teenaged boy who hardly seemed old enough for such work.

John described the memorable undertaking they experienced that Tuesday:

*The day was a beautiful one for traveling, and the massive hills and mountains of Chekiang quite too beautiful for words. To get out of the province we had one mountain pass to climb. The journey was not bad from our side as far as climbing up went, but bad going down, almost two miles from the top to the bottom. Betty walked up the way from which we came, which was only a short walk, and then walked a little way down when she saw what the other side looked like, preferring to walk down rather than to slide out of the chair.*

*However, she took to the chair again, and believe me I prayed! Two carriers like that and such a descent. In places where the path doubled back on itself, the front man would be down one "flight of stairs" and the back one up them, with Betty in the chair hanging over the "abyss below." I walked right close back of the rear man, and once threw my stick away and grabbed for the poles when he slipped a bit. I breathed a great sigh of relief when we were at the bottom. It was a long and hard day, from 7:30 A.M. till 7:00 P.M.*[7]

Two days later they boarded a boat destined for their home in Suancheng. After their exhausting travels on foot, the couple relished the opportunity to spend a day reading and napping as the boat carried them smoothly along to their home by that night.

# twenty-one

By the time John and Betty arrived back in Suancheng they had come to the joyous realization that Betty was carrying a child. She wrote to her parents, sharing the happy news, along with a description of the itineration they had just completed. Clara Scott wrote back a worried letter, airing her concern that nothing short of a miracle could prevent Betty from having trouble with her pregnancy after such a rigorous journey. Betty, however, insisted that she was probably in better health as a result of the travels.

One week after returning to Suancheng, John and Betty participated in the annual regional church conference held there. Christians gathered from area congregations for the meetings, which were held three times daily for a week. An American Presbyterian missionary named James Graham and a Chinese evangelist, Mr. Han, were the guest speakers. Graham had been raised in

China and spoke the language like a native.

Betty reported to John's parents after the meetings: "Mr. Graham and Mr. Han gave splendid messages here. Beginning with 'Who Is Jesus Christ?' they went through the fundamental doctrines of the Bible, not forgetting the original and fallen states of man, the meaning of the cross, the victorious Christian life, the Second Coming, and the final destiny of all creation and human beings. It was all good, solid truth, and the messages were powerful.

"Many outsiders, including prominent men of the city, came in, and the meetings grew in size. No matter what the general subject was, every meeting ended with a clear presentation of the Gospel, whether or not a definite invitation was given."[1]

The following week, on Wednesday, March 21, John traveled twenty miles southeast of Suancheng to Kinghsien. He had been asked by missionary Sam Warren to help with a series of meetings similar to the ones held in Suancheng. In the past Warren had been stationed in Kinghsien, and he was still called on occasionally to assist the national leaders who now led the work there without the aid of a resident missionary.

As a testimony of the progress that John was making in the language, he was invited to be the featured speaker at the Kinghsien meetings. He and Pastor Ho, with whom John had worked in the children's ministry of the Suancheng church, were asked to share the same messages which James Graham and Mr. Han had preached at the previous week's conference. This they happily did, with John speaking each morning and evening.

Attendance was noticeably lower at the Kinghsien conference than in Suancheng, especially during the daytime when only twenty to thirty people came to the various sessions. However, the numbers swelled considerably at the evening services when more people were free to participate.

After the Kinghsien conference the missionaries and Pastor Ho visited three outstations in the area where they shared the Gospel in chapel services and open-air gatherings. At the final outstation in Nan Uan, they had a profitable and interesting set of meetings with members of the extended Song clan.

Bandits were active in the area. Once, two Song children had been kidnapped and nearly a thousand dollars had had to be paid for their ransom. Consequently, at the nighttime meetings some of the men came with their rifles. Two or three of the armed men would stand in back of the attentive crowd and anytime a dog barked outside they would slip outside to see who was approaching.

Commented John afterward, "Really, some of the pictures these fellows presented were most incongruous, such as one fellow stomping up the aisle with a gun in one hand and a hymnbook in the other. And another, the schoolteacher, fur cap on head, several top teeth missing, a gun over one shoulder, and a baby in the opposite arm."[2]

After two days of ministry among the many Song families and in the villages scattered around that plain, the evangelists left for home on Friday, March 30. Before leaving, however, they needed to attend a feast, so they were not able to get underway until early afternoon. John hurried ahead on his own, desiring to traverse the nearly thirty miles back to Suancheng by day's end. He was anxious to get back to Betty who had been left alone. (The Birches were in Wuhu where Grace had just given birth to another son, John Alfred.) He arrived home about ten that night.

Three weeks later John set out again for southern Anhwei Province. He was eager to minister once again in that region, where they intended to move later in the year, before the oppressive summer heat set in. He first made his way back to the home of the Li family in Kuan In Ch'iao where he and Betty had enjoyed a pleasant visit during their itineration earlier that year. This time, however, John ran headlong into a bitter domestic dispute. He related the sad story in a letter to friends and family members along with the request that they pray about the grievous situation:

*The old father in the Li family had originally arranged a marriage for his second son with one of the local families. The lad grew up with the girl, went to school with her, and looked forward to marrying her. When the time came, the old man changed his mind (probably for money reasons) and married him off to another young girl in the neighborhood. The lad was heartbroken, but there was nothing to be done but to take the girl his father had arranged for him to marry.*

*Undoubtedly he never gave that girl a chance from the beginning, for he didn't want her. The result has been that she reacted as badly as could be expected, and has turned out to be sulky, lazy, bad tempered, etc.—and very little wonder, either. She probably is not as bright nor as capable as the other two daughters-in-law in that household. But things might have been different had she had a chance.*

*The result has been revilings on both sides
and beatings. And the Lis were on the verge of a
lawsuit with the girl's father at the time I
arrived on the scene. I didn't know this till later,
but the atmosphere of that home did give me a
most troubled weekend. As these folk have a different dialect, I couldn't even get the whole of
the story until later on. But I knew where their
trouble lay and, though not knowing how far the
matter had gone, I could give them Ephesians
five on the duties of husbands and wives.*

*Friends and the village elders suggest send-
ing the girl back to her father, who is willing to
take her. But she declares she will not go, saying that while she lives she is a member of their
family, and will ever be a "family spirit" (to
plague them if they mistreat her) after she is
dead. So they will not force her to go home with
such a threat.*

*From a human point of view they are incom-
patible, but that leaves out the transforming
power of God in the lives of men. Will not some
of you friends take this family to God in prayer?
For if, or rather when, that young man and his
wife are really happy together, that valley will
have one of the strongest possible testimonies to
the grace of God.[3]*

The following Monday John traveled on to Miaosheo
where he thoroughly enjoyed staying with Mrs. Wang.
"When I'm at Mrs. Wang's," he told his family members, "I'm in real clover, for she keeps the place very
clean and cooks excellent meals. She knows what the

foreigner likes and what's good for him. She just hovers over you like the dear old grandmother she is.

"After coming from the Li home with all its squabbles, it was delightful to come here and see the way mother-in-law and daughter-in-law get on together. It was very beautiful, for instance, to see the younger woman run off to get a wrap to throw about the older woman one evening when it began to grow cold. It spoke volumes for mutual love and respect. Here was one time where a match arranged by the parents was working out splendidly."[4]

John was joined in his ministry at Miaosheo by a native evangelist named Lo Ke-chou. Lo had carried out fruitful evangelistic work in the vicinity of Kinghsien, and it was intended that he would move with his family to Miaosheo later in the year to assist the Stams in their new ministry in that region. John and he spent ten days there, visiting in the homes of the church members, most of whom were scattered around the countryside. They went to a number of nearby villages to preach, distribute tracts, and sell printed copies of the Gospels. On rainy days they found it most profitable to stay in Miaosheo itself as, with little to do, the shopkeepers were very willing to listen to their testimony.

The evangelists next went to Tsingteh to be there on the city's large annual market day. One day each year everyone from the surrounding areas who had anything he hoped to sell or buy came to the town. The streets were packed with people, and big theatrical productions visited the city.

"The day is specially valuable to us," John explained, "in that we can get the printed word into the hands of people from over a great section of the surrounding country. Four of us, two foreigners and two Chinese, separated through the town, and getting to some place where the crowd was not too thick, passed out tracts and sold Gospels for many hours that day. We sold many hundreds of Gospels and distributed thousands of tracts."[5]

The highlight of that particular itineration came at the next community they visited, Peh Ti, which was located south of Tsingteh. Though Sam Warren had never had the opportunity to minister there, he had asked friends in England and Australia to pray for the town in anticipation of the Gospel's being taken there in the future. John and Mr. Lo went there now to spend part of two days and one night. The missionary afterward related the happy results:

"From the first it was evident that this town was a prepared place. I've never seen such friendliness and such courteous interest. The young students were first to gather around, and were quick to learn to sing our choruses. That brought more students, the schoolteacher, and the local official. All were very cordial and sympathetic. That night we had a most attentive audience in our inn which stood for an hour and a half and didn't seem to want to go home."[6]

The evangelists shared the same basic Gospel message a second and then a third time, but still few of their listeners offered to leave. "We finally had to end by announcing that we had to go to bed," reported John.

The next morning as John and Mr. Lo left town to go pay a brief visit to a neighboring village, two children came running after them, shouting, "Buy a book! Buy a book!"

The men turned and called back to the children, "Don't worry. We'll be back for dinner. You can buy a book then."

But the children kept right on after them. They feared that the men were leaving for good and that they would not have another opportunity to purchase a copy of the book that contained wonderful news of a Savior. One of the children, a girl, actually began to cry.

"Such was their anxiety," John later related, "that we had to turn in our tracks and sell the little girl a book or leave her wailing and weeping."

The missionaries met with a sharply contrasting reception in the next community they visited, Kiang Ts'uen. "One of the young men seemed to be a bit of a jokester," related John of the uncomfortable experience, "and of course there are things about the foreigner and the way he brings his message that can be turned into a laugh. I seemed almost bound so that I couldn't preach the Gospel as I would have in other places. A laughing crowd, with the laugh turned on you, is the hardest to speak to.

"However," he added more hopefully, "we sold some seventy Gospels and left many tracts in that town. Do pray for these silent messengers. They aren't so frail as we and don't mind being laughed at quite so much."[7]

John, Mr. Lo, and Sam Warren visited three other towns east of Tsingteh before returning home. At one of those, Hu Loh Si, they encountered opposition from five government schoolteachers who instructed their students not to receive the Christians' tracts and taught them to sing a chorus that proclaimed, "Down with Jesus."

That evening the evangelists held their usual meeting in front of the inn where they were staying. Children from two private schools in town were there, as were the city's tradespeople. The students from the government school came to create a disturbance by tearing up tracts and trying to pull some of their peers away from the

170

gathering. But they failed in their attempts to disrupt the meeting as the crowd remained quiet and attentive.

At the conclusion of this trip, John wrote to supporters in the United States: "We are looking forward with great expectations to our new field. It's a great open door, with its many villages scattered all through our parish of more than two hundred square miles, and we look to God to use us for His glory. Adversaries?—Yes, you know our great adversary. Besides him there is the same awful indifference that you have to face at home. Added to that there's superstition among the ignorant and a type of nationalism among the educated young folk that scorns foreigners for everything except science and machines."[8]

# twenty-two

About six weeks later, early in July of 1934, John and Betty moved temporarily to Wuhu. Their main purpose for going there was so that John could take over the duties of the CIM's local secretary, a Mr. Walton. The secretary and his wife wanted to get away to the mountains for a much-needed two-month reprieve from the heavy responsibilities he routinely bore. Another advantage to being in Wuhu was that they were close to a hospital when the time came for Betty to give birth.

That the job of secretary was not an ideal fit for John is readily apparent in private letters to family members back home. On July 18 he wrote: "I'm very glad now that I did take up bookkeeping in [business college], but I like it no better than ever. The local secretary's work here requires a lot of pen work, and I never did specially like juggling figures through cash books, journals, and ledgers. I like handling men and things much better

172

than pens and figures.

"However, the dear chap who holds this job down here for us all through the year certainly deserves our thanks. He's as truly a missionary as we are, keeping us supplied with money, food, etc., and he won't lose his reward. He's a very obliging fellow, and spends much of his time running around on errands for us that make things much more endurable when we go inland."[1]

Similarly, on August 2 he revealed: "I'm glad I'm not designated for work in a place like this. The local secretary's work does take time—bookkeeping, meeting boats, buying supplies, etc. And while the house is in a lovely location, it is too far away from the town itself for purposes of the work (real spiritual). They've asked me to preach in church on Sunday, for which I am thankful."[2]

In addition to carrying out secretarial responsibilities, John joined Betty that summer in continuing their diligent study of the language. Toward the end of July Betty wrote, "John is studying faithfully every day, besides doing office work as it turns up." By the close of the next month Betty successfully completed the fourth and final set of major language exams the CIM required of its women missionaries.

Much of Anhwei Province experienced a drought that summer. Weeks on end passed with no rain, reducing crop yields to half or less than half of normal levels. In Wuhu people suffered through sweltering temperatures of over one hundred degrees in the shade. "It's a bit hotter here than in Suancheng," John related in a correspondence, "but there are compensations like electric lights, fans that you can run all night, ice and ice cream, all of which, while expensive, are well worth it."[3]

The young missionary couple felt blessed to have a

Christian native named Mei Tsong-fuh begin working as their hired household servant that summer. She had once been married but her husband had abandoned her, and she now needed a means of making a livelihood.

Mei was hospitalized in Wuhu for treatment of a serious infection in both her eyes. One of her eyes was so bad that it needed to be taken out and replaced with a glass eye, but the infection in the other eye was cleared up with proper medical attention.

After her release from the hospital, she began working for John and Betty, who assisted in paying her medical bills. The arrangement worked out well, and plans were made for her to move to Tsingteh with them later in the year.

On Thursday, September 6, Betty entered the hospital at the doctor's suggestion, and two days later John informed family members: "The doctor wants her to get a good rest before things begin, which might be any minute by the way. Incidentally, they want her to stay there for three weeks after [the delivery] to give her heart a good rest before getting around again. The doctor is a bit careful about that heart, which is another call for all our earnest prayers.

"However, she is very comfortable up there. The hospital is on a high bluff above the river, and from the porch outside her room she can look way up and down the river. Really it is a most ideal spot for a hospital, and we are thankful to have such a place here. I go up to see her twice a day on my bike. The Waltons are back tomorrow, which will relieve me of all responsibilities for the house and the secretarial work."[4]

The following Tuesday, September 11, 1934, Betty gave birth to a healthy baby daughter at 3:15 in the afternoon. Weighing six pounds, eleven ounces at birth, the infant was named Helen Priscilla Stam.

It was nearly a month later—October 8—before the cautious doctor released Betty and the baby to return home from the hospital. Two weeks after that she wrote a letter to John's parents telling them about their newest grandchild:

"The baby looks like John, nearly everybody says at first sight. She has his mouth and rather pointed chin. Her eyes are a deep blue and very big. Her face is so sweet and round, with a lot of dark hair which is actually curly when damp.

"It is a real joy to take care of her. We can't say she never cries. But during the night she sleeps soundly from 10 P.M. to 6 A.M., and most of the time from 6 A.M. to 10 P.M., too.

"She won't keep her arms inside the bedclothes, so I pile on an extra knitted jacket. Last night she howled and kicked so hard that she put her feet right through a little flannelette gown which Mother Scott had made for her! I'm afraid it was temper. For the minute anybody picks her up, she is as placid and serene as can be, with a slightly reproachful expression, as much as to say, 'Why didn't you come sooner?' So we shall have to be very strict with her."[5]

Clara Scott traveled from Tsinan to assist Betty with Helen for two weeks. They were also delighted to receive a three-day visit from Betty's newlywed sister, Bunny (Beatrice), who along with her husband, Theodore Stevenson, was just arriving in China to begin missionary service under the Presbyterian Board, U.S.A.

On Friday, October 19, John set out again for southern Anhwei. This time he was accompanied by fellow CIM missionary Erwin Kohfield who served in Tunki, about thirty miles south of Tsingteh. Kohfield's was the nearest station to where John and Betty would be settling, and the two men hoped to work together in developing the churches in both their locales.

Late in September the Kohfields had been forced to flee Tunki when Communist soldiers suddenly crossed the border from Kiangsi Province to the south and invaded the town in search of food and foreigners. Erwin, his wife, Mary, and their three young children spent part of one night in hiding on a nearby mountain. Stealing back to the city, Erwin learned that the Communist force had already moved on, and he returned at midnight to retrieve his family members. As they made their way back to town through the dark, however, Mary fell over a bank. She was carrying their baby at the time, and the infant's head was bruised in the fall.

CIM officials immediately brought the Kohfields to Suancheng where they had stayed the past three weeks. Now John and Erwin intended to scout out conditions in the region to determine the advisability of returning there to minister with their families.

They found the region hard hit by the drought. Everywhere they went crop yields had been only one-quarter to one-half of normal production. Food would be in short supply for the residents of the region during the upcoming winter. The food scarcity was compounded by the presence of thousands of troops moving about in the region, all needing to be fed as well.

After Communist forces entered southern Anhwei, the governor of the province went to the vicinity of Tunki with a contingent of ten thousand soldiers. Reportedly he was there not only to prevent further Communist incursions into the area, but also to keep an eye on a former governor of the province who, along with his twenty thousand troops, was stationed south of Tunki. This former governor was a notorious turncoat who was suspected of secretly aiding the Communists. The present governor had fortified Tunki with some thirty stone forts and apparently was serious about defending the southern border of his province from further military threats.

In Tsingteh the two missionaries met with the district magistrate, Mr. Peng. When John asked about conditions in the area, the official at first responded, "We're having some trouble with small groups of bandits in the district due to the drought and shortage of food."

"Then we had better not come down for awhile with our families," John suggested.

"I would agree with you," affirmed the magistrate.

"We certainly would not want to risk a meeting with Communists," stated John.

"Oh, no, no!" Mr. Peng responded emphatically. "There is no danger of Communists here. As far as that is concerned, you may come at once and bring your family. I will guarantee your safety, and if there should be any trouble, you can come to my yamen."

Their discussion with the district magistrate in Tunki was equally reassuring. "There will be no further trouble here with the governor's troops nearby," he confidently predicted. "You and your family can safely return. We will assure your protection."

On the basis of such assurances, the Stams and Kohfields were given permission by CIM officials to proceed with their families to southern Anhwei. The Kohfields returned to Tunki shortly after John and Erwin completed their investigative trip. John and Betty spent several days in Suancheng helping out with the short-term

Bible school that was being held there just then, packing up their belongings, and saying good-bye to the many friends they had come to cherish during their year of residence there.

Their final Sunday in Suancheng, November 18, a special child dedication service was held. John and Betty dedicated Helen to the Lord, and the Birches did the same with their infant son, John. When the officiating minister, Rev. Harold Weller, a missionary from Anking, prayed for Helen Priscilla, he asked that she might grow to be like Priscilla in the Bible, a help to the church and a minister to the saints.

"It was very impressive, and very blessed," John wrote of the service to family members. "Both babies behaved wonderfully, our little Helen, when she was awake, quite enjoying herself doing nothing."[6]

# twenty-three

John and Betty had their household goods transported on five wheelbarrows the seventy miles from Suancheng to Tsingteh. On Thursday, November 22, 1934, they set out for southern Anhwei by bus. Rather than ride on an overcrowded public passenger bus, they were able to find seats on one the military had chartered to transport two large guns and a mere eight soldiers. The trip took only three hours as the bus was able to roll right past the red flags that signaled public buses to stop at numerous small wayside stations.

The couple was blessed with beautiful weather the next day as they walked from where the bus line ended, over two mountain passes, and along a vast valley into Tsingteh. Shortly after that the weather turned rainy and considerably colder.

Two days after the missionaries' arrival, on Sunday, November 25, they had their first church service. The service was attended by their household servants, one of the carriers whom they had hired, a visiting Christian from a neighboring outstation, two unbelievers from the community who drifted in for only a few minutes, and one young girl from the neighborhood. The missionaries and their servants were the only ones present at the church service the first Sunday in December.

John shared this news with his relatives on December 5: "I have opened the street chapel some five nights since being here and have had fairly attentive audiences. Do be praying for us. We are certainly at the beginning of things here. The people here seem quite friendly. Several men have been in with whom I have been able to have a good talk. God help us to open the Scriptures to them."[1]

On that same day he wrote another letter to friends back home: "Things are always happening otherwise than one expects. The Lord help us to be quite satisfied, whatever He sends our way this day. Whether our hopes for study or work are realized or not, may He help us be satisfied with His plan for the day, as He unfolds it to us.

"Talk about being a 'spectacle'! The Chinese has it (and rightly so from the original text [1 Corinthians 4:9]) that we are made to be like a theatrical play, at which others come to look. If ever you get to the foreign field you will know what that means. All that you wear and eat, all that you do and say comes in for the closest scrutiny and not a little comment. Hence the special need for prayer that God will help His missionaries to shine for Him every hour."[2]

Those words took on a sort of prophetic significance in light of the unforeseen developments that the young missionary couple encountered beginning the very next day, Thursday, December 6. Early that morning, moving swiftly and silently along unfrequented mountain paths, Communist troops crossed over the border from Kiangsi Province into southern Anhwei. Undetected by government forces some sixty miles to the south and east, two thousand Red soldiers attacked and quickly overpowered helpless Tsingteh. Within hours the size of the Red army had swelled to six thousand.

The Communists immediately took over the city's yamen, killing three officials who served there. They looted the town, taking the people's food, money, and other valuables. No houses were burned, but the forts on the city wall were torn down and two gaping breaches were made in the wall.

The Reds killed fourteen of Tsingteh's headmen, each the leader of a group of ten families. In addition to incarcerating John, Betty, and Helen, they took more than twenty other prisoners, a few women, and a number of wealthy citizens, whom they held for ransom. The Chinese women, none of whom were violated, were later released. Some of the wealthy citizens were eventually killed while others were set free.

Reportedly, as part of their cruelty, the soldiers discussed openly in front of John and Betty whether or not they should kill their infant out of hand so as not to be troubled with her. When it began to appear that such an atrocity might be carried out, an objection was raised by an anonymous onlooker.

Nothing was known about the man except that he was a farmer who had been imprisoned in the local yamen when the Red army arrived in town. The Communists had released him as well as the other prisoners when they took over the yamen. Now they were incensed to hear him protest, "Certainly the baby has done nothing worthy of death."

"Then it's your life for hers!" the soldiers threatened angrily.

"I am willing," the unidentified farmer quietly responded. As a result, his life was taken and Helen was allowed to go on living.

Around four the next morning the Communists left Tsingteh with the missionaries and other captives. They marched the twelve miles over mountain roads to Miaosheo. John carried Helen on his back. Mercifully, Betty was allowed to ride a horse part of the way.

Ironically, John had arranged to meet Evangelist Lo in Miaosheo later that day, Friday, December 7, so that they could carry out some evangelistic work there. Knowing nothing of the tragic developments in Tsingteh, the native evangelist, along with his wife and four-year-old son, had arrived in Miaosheo the previous evening and spent the night in Mrs. Wang's home.

At nine o'clock Friday morning an advance guard of soldiers was seen entering the city. Not knowing whether they were government or Communist troops, the younger women and children in Mrs. Wang's house (her son, Wang Shi-ho, and his family lived with her) were sent to the foot of the mountain on the outskirts of town as a precautionary measure. Lo and Wang cautiously made their way toward the main street in order to investigate further.

The Reds were again searching for the city's headmen. Someone pointed in the direction of Lo and Wang, stating, "There is one."

Wang immediately fled, for he was, indeed, a headman. Lo, however, stood his ground and was taken into custody.

"Are you a headman?" a Communist officer demanded of him. "How many men belong to your local militia? How many rifles do you have here in the city?"

Remaining calm, Lo responded, "I am a stranger to this town, I arrived here only last night."

"Do you know anyone here in town who can verify what you're telling me?" the officer asked.

Lo led him and a squadron of soldiers to the house of Chang Hsiu-sheng, a doctor in town who belonged to the Miaosheo church. Chang truthfully stated of the evangelist, "This man arrived in town last night. He is of the same trade as I, heals diseases and distributes tracts in the country."

The army officer apparently did not associate tract distribution with Christian activity, for he seemed satisfied with the identification. Instead, he said to Lo, "It is all well, then. You are free to go."

Lo bowed politely and slowly walked away. When he reached a back street, he quickened his pace and joined Wang, their wives, and children at the base of the mountain. They all climbed the mountain where they would spend the next two days and nights.

The rest of the Red army arrived in Miaosheo with John and Betty and their other prisoners sometime later that day. As the soldiers pillaged the town, they left the missionaries under the supervision of the local postmaster.

"Where are they taking you?" queried the postal official. "Where are you going?"

"We do not know where they are going," replied John confidently, "but we are going to heaven."

The kindly man offered them some fruit to eat. Betty, having the baby to nurse, gladly accepted. John declined, choosing instead to write another brief letter to CIM officials in Shanghai. He left the correspondence with the postmaster, asking him to see that it was delivered.

*Miaosheo, Anhwei*
*December 7, 1934*

*China Inland Mission*
*Dear Brethren,*

*We are in the hands of the Communists here, being taken from Tsingteh when they passed through yesterday. I tried to persuade them to let my wife and baby go back to Tsingteh with a letter to you, but they wouldn't let her, and so we both made the trip to Miaosheo today, my wife traveling part of the way on a horse.*

*They want $20,000 before they will free us, which we have told them we are sure will not be paid. Famine relief money and our personal money and effects are all in their hands.*

*God give you wisdom in what you do and give us grace and fortitude. He is able.*

*Yours in Him,*
*John C. Stam*[3]

That evening they were taken to a deserted home that had once belonged to a wealthy family. They were placed in an inner room of the house while soldiers stood guard outside the door. John was tied in a standing position to the bedpost. Betty was left unbound so that she could attend to the baby.

That same night another group of soldiers stayed in Mrs. Wang's home. She was unaware that John and Betty were being held as prisoners in the town. While the soldiers did not harm her physically, when they left the next day they took nearly her entire harvest of rice, and what they did not carry away they dumped in the pond just outside her house.

She stayed up all night making puffed rice to take to her loved ones on the mountain. Early on Saturday morning she set out to find them. She had great difficulty in walking because her legs were swollen from disease and the mountain was very steep. As she went along she began to weep because she could not locate her relatives. Finally someone found her and was able to guide her to them.

She discovered a group of about fifteen refugees huddled together. Although they had only one wadded quilt to share among them, they had not dared to light a fire lest it be spotted by the invading soldiers. One man in their party had a sickle that he used to cut some grass so that they could cover themselves at night. Their only available food was wild chestnuts.

A rumor carried by other refugees had reached the little group on the mountain that a foreigner was being held captive by the Reds. Lo thought it might be the priest from Tsingteh's Roman Catholic church. He hoped that John and Betty had been able to escape from the city in time.

Shortly before ten o'clock Saturday morning, December 8, the Communist soldiers, having decided to execute John and Betty, came and ordered them to strip down to their long underwear. After tying the missionaries' hands tightly behind their backs with rope, they marched the couple out into the street. John walked along barefoot while Betty wore a pair of socks he had given to her to help protect her feet. Their baby was left behind, completely unattended, in the empty house.

As the soldiers marched the missionaries through the

city streets, they ordered the townspeople to come and witness the execution of the "foreign devils." Only one man, Chang Hsiu-sheng, the medicine seller, dared to speak up in behalf of the couple. Chang had always been a rather lukewarm member of the Miaosheo church, but now he fell on his knees before the soldiers and pleaded for John and Betty's release.

The outraged soldiers bound him also, accusing him of being in union with the foreigners. When a search was made of his home a short time later, his Bible and hymnal were discovered, providing tangible evidence that he was a practicing Christian. The Communists took Chang with them as a prisoner when they left Miaosheo late that night, then killed him at the next village they invaded.

At the end of Miaosheo's main street, just outside of town, stood Eagle Hill. There, in order to justify the executions that were about to take place, the Communists harangued the cowed townspeople concerning the evils of foreigners and their influence.

Presently John was ordered to kneel. He did so on one knee and spoke a few words to his captors. The local residents were not standing near enough to hear what he said. Suddenly and savagely one of the soldiers stepped forward and slashed his throat with a large knife. The missionary's lifeless body crumpled forward to the ground.

The witnessing crowd saw Betty shudder then drop to her knees. A moment later a large sword flashed through the air and struck through the back of her neck, killing her instantly.

Shortly afterward the soldiers returned to town, leaving the bodies of the missionaries where they had fallen in a grove of pine trees on the hill. Miaosheo's citizens silently stole back to their homes, filled with horror and sorrow.

# *twenty-four*

Even as the Communist soldiers were leading John and Betty up Eagle Hill to be executed, government troops were arriving in the vicinity of Miaosheo. About noon the government force opened fire on the Red soldiers, most of whom were in position in a low wooded ridge just outside the town. Government troops continued their attack throughout the afternoon, but it was largely ineffective, with only one or two Communist soldiers being killed. The Reds returned little gunfire, and when the shooting stopped both armies were still in their original positions.

Later that night, around ten o'clock, the Communists withdrew from Miaosheo, setting fire to houses along the road as they left. They moved on three miles to the next sizeable town.

Earlier that day another refugee fleeing Miaosheo had brought word to Evangelist Lo and his party on the

187

mountain of John and Betty's tragic deaths. The next morning, Sunday, December 9, the small band of Christians crept back down the mountain and into the city.

Lo immediately began to inquire about the location of John and Betty's bodies. Some people would not tell him anything, fearing that the Communist soldiers, still only a short distance away, might return and punish them for siding with foreigners. The townspeople supposed that there were likely still spies among them who sympathized with the Communists.

At last Lo learned that the bodies were on Eagle Hill. As he hurried up the street toward the spot, an old woman approached him and informed him that there was also a foreign baby left deserted in one of the homes. After she pointed out the house to him, he immediately went there.

Upon entering the home, he heard Helen crying and found her in the inner room where her parents had been forced to leave her a full twenty-four hours earlier. She still lay on the bed, warmly snuggled in the infant sleeping bag she had been left in. Pinned inside the layers of clothes were two five-dollar bills that Betty had secretly placed there with the prayerful hope that someone would discover the baby and use the money to provide for her needs.

Taking the infant with him, Lo continued on to Eagle Hill. He was so shocked by the grievous sight that at first he could hardly bring himself to look at the corpses. Then, hastening back into town, he left the baby in the care of his wife and went to purchase a pair of coffins on credit. He also bought four white sheets to wrap the bodies in and, in keeping with Chinese custom, a supply of lime to put in the coffins.

The evangelist next returned to Eagle Hill with Mrs. Wang, her son, and a handful of poor people who had been hired to help with the care of the bodies. Birds were seen starting to circle overhead in the sky and a number of dogs were lurking nearby, but, thankfully, Lo and his companions arrived in time so that the corpses were not in any way desecrated.

The peasants were paid to reattach the heads, which had been nearly completely severed from the torsos, using hemp thread. As that was done, the little group could not help but notice that John's face bore an expression of unmistakable joy, while Betty's facial features reflected complete serenity. After the three Christians had lovingly wrapped the bodies in the sheets and placed them in the coffins, they knelt in prayer.

A crowd had gathered to watch them. The local citizens expressed deepest sorrow and regret over the deaths of the young couple. Some even went so far as publicly to curse the Communists for their heinous crime.

When Lo had finished praying, he stood and addressed the crowd with great fervor: "You have seen these wounded bodies, and you pity these foreigners for their suffering and death. But you should know that they are children of God. Their spirits are unharmed and at this minute are in the presence of God.

"They came to China and to Miaosheo not for themselves but for you, to tell you about God and His love, that you might believe in the Lord Jesus Christ and be saved eternally. You have heard this message. Remember it is true. Their death proves that. Do not forget what they told you. Repent and believe the Gospel."

Many of the listeners wept as Lo spoke. Of that unusual reaction, George Birch later commented:

"Personally I have not seen weeping in response to a Gospel message in China. Why the change? Why the melted hearts? They had witnessed a demonstration of the power of God and the truth of the Gospel. We expect much fruit from the glorious death and the faithful testimony of these two shining ones."

Hearing rumors that the Communists were about to return to Miaosheo, Lo was at a loss over what to do. His fragile young son had become deathly ill through the two nights of exposure out on the mountain and was in no shape to travel. But if the Communists returned, he and his whole family would be in grave danger, having actively shown concern for the foreigners. Also, Helen needed to be delivered safely to missionaries who could assume care of her.

Lo and his wife set out on foot for Kinghsien in the north, the town where they had been living and assisting with evangelistic work. They hired a coolie who carried Lo's son and baby Helen in rice baskets at opposite ends of a long pole. The infant slept peacefully, but the little boy's condition became increasingly grave. He did not eat anything or speak a single word that entire day.

The next day, Tuesday, Lo was able to hire sedan chairs to transport them the remainder of the distance to Kinghsien. To the great relief and joy of Lo and his wife, that day their son's condition improved immensely. He even sat up in his basket and sang a hymn. The parents, who had previously experienced the sorrow of losing two baby girls, heartily praised God for sparing the life of their son.

The Los found native women who were willing to nurse Helen at their various stops along the way to Kinghsien. Once they arrived there they were able to buy powdered milk with some of the money Betty had left concealed in the baby's clothing. After that, Mrs. Lo fed her from a bottle on a regular three-hour schedule.

"I am quite sure," George Birch remarked afterward, "that there is not another woman in all that district who could have looked after baby Helen as Mrs. Lo did. Her baby boy had been born in the Methodist Hospital in Wuhu, and she still had the bottle he had used."

Meanwhile, as Lo was seeking to get Helen back to missionary acquaintances, delayed news of the troubles in southern Anhwei finally began to reach CIM officials who were attending China Council meetings in Shanghai. The first unconfirmed report of a Communist attack arrived in the capital on Monday evening, December 10. The next day a confirmed report was received saying that the Reds had attacked Tsingteh and that John and Betty had been taken captive.

CIM representatives promptly began conferring with high-level Chinese officials to learn more about the situation and to determine what could be done to effect the release of the captured missionary couple. Due to the confusion caused by the fighting and the poor lines of communication in China at that time, new and reliable reports came at a maddeningly slow rate.

News of John and Betty's capture as well as the uncertainty over little Helen's welfare and whereabouts was immediately telegraphed to Christians in various parts of the world. Believers in several countries began to pray earnestly for their protection and release.

On Thursday, December 13, W. J. Hanna, the CIM superintendent for Anhwei Province, received a letter from the Wuhu Magistrate informing him that John and Betty's bodies had been found at Miaosheo. The next

191

day a knock came at the door of George Birch's missionary residence in Suancheng. It took him a moment to recognize the weary woman standing before him in muddy clothes as Mrs. Lo.

Unable to restrain her tears, she extended a bundle to him and said brokenly, "This is all we have left."

George assumed that her husband must have been killed by the Communists and that this was her small young son. Loosening the shawl around the child, however, the missionary was astounded to look into the beautiful sleeping face of Helen Stam. A moment later, having settled accounts with the chair coolies, Mr. Lo came in and related a full account of the past week's events to the missionary.

The following day, Saturday, Helen was taken to the Wuhu hospital where she was found to be in excellent health. She still had her placid disposition and slept peacefully through each night. In light of her remarkable deliverance and preservation, she came to be dubbed, first by the missionaries in China, and then by Christians around the world, "The Miracle Baby."

# twenty-five

Immediately after receiving news of John and Betty's deaths, the CIM telegraphed its heartfelt condolences to both sets of their parents. Peter Stam responded: "Deeply appreciate your consolation. Sacrifice seems great, but not too great for Him Who gave Himself for us. Experiencing God's grace. Believe wholeheartedly Romans 8:28."[1]

About that same time he wrote the following to other friends and acquaintances:

> Our dear children, John C. Stam and Elisabeth Scott Stam, have gone to be with the Lord. They loved Him, they served Him, and now they are with Him. What could be more glorious? It is true, the manner in which they were sent out of this world was a shock to us all, but whatever of suffering they may have endured is now past,

*and they are both infinitely blessed with the joys of Heaven.*

*As for those of us who have been left behind, we were once more reminded of our sacred vows by a telegram received from one of John's schoolmates in the Midwest— "Remember, you gave John to God, not to China." Our hearts, though bowed for a little while with sadness, answered, "Amen!" It was our desire that he, as well as we, should serve the Lord, and if that could be better done by death than by life, we would have it so. The sacrifice may seem great now, but no sacrifice is too great to make for Him Who gave Himself for us.*

*We are earnestly praying that it will all be for God's glory and the salvation of souls. How glad we shall be if through this dreadful experience many souls shall be won for the Lord Jesus! How glad we shall be if many dear Christian young people shall be inspired to give themselves to the Lord as never before, for a life of sacrifice and service!*

*We were honored by having sons and daughters minister for our Lord among the heathen, but we are more signally honored that two of them have won the martyr's crown. We are sure that our dear brother and sister, Dr. and Mrs. Charles E. Scott, both join us in saying, "The Lord gave, and the Lord hath taken away; blessed be the name of the Lord" [Job 1:21].*[2]

That same tone of triumphant faith is clearly heard in Clara Scott's letter, written to friends two days after learning of John and Betty's deaths:

*We have been thankful that from the first we com-
mitted our three precious ones into the Lord's
hands, and have prayed that His name might be
glorified and His will done. We have, of course,
prayed that, if it be in accordance with His plans
for them, their lives might be spared to witness to
His great power to release from physical danger.
But at the same time we, if His name could be the
more glorified through the sacrifice of their
young lives, were still willing to give up our trea-
sure into His hands, knowing that He would not
carry out such a purpose unless the greater glory
would result through their death than through
their living witness.*

*When the telegram came Thursday evening
saying that Betty and John were with the Lord
we did not mourn as those who have no hope,
but could not but feel that a great blessing might
come to the cause of Christ here in China and
also wherever their martyrdom might be known.
We cannot but rejoice that they have been
accounted worthy to suffer for His sake, and we
cannot be sorry for them that thus early they
have been released from all earthly trials and
have entered into the glory provided for those
who belong wholly to Him.*

*They are not the ones to have sought release
from working longer in this world of darkness,
but the Lord must have been satisfied that their
work here was completed, and that their
willingness to die for Him will bring in a larger*

*harvest of souls than as if they had lived many
years longer. It has been brought to our hearts
by many Chinese and foreign friends that the
kernel of wheat that dies will bear much fruit—
that it cannot fall to the ground in vain, and that
two kernels will bear more fruit than one.*

Concerning the deliverance of her granddaughter,
Clara added:

*To me it is nothing less than a miracle that Baby
Helen Priscilla has been spared. My husband
said this morning, "All the hordes of wicked
Communists couldn't harm that helpless babe,
if it were the Lord's purpose to have her live to
glorify His name and show His power." We
know that even more He could have delivered
Betty and John from their captors, had that been
His will for them.[3]*

Hundreds of expressions of consolation flowed in
from all over the world to both sets of bereaved parents.
In a single mail the Scotts received letters of comfort from
Australia, New Zealand, Arabia, Hong Kong, Germany,
Sweden, England, Canada, and the United States.

"We want to express our deepest gratitude," wrote
Peter Stam, "to the many friends in Christ who have
leaped to our support in this hour of trouble. Some may
be wondering if our faith has been shaken. Praise God, it
has not. Indeed, it has been greatly strengthened by the
many portions of the Word of God which have been sent
to encourage us. They poured in by letter and by telegram and by telephone. We thank God, too, for the dear

Christian friends who came to us in our grief and clasped our hands and whispered verses of Scripture into our ears."[4]

Several memorial services were held in both China and the United States to honor John and Betty and to praise God for their lives of consecrated service. After the bodies of the two slain missionaries were retrieved from Miaosheo and brought to Wuhu, a memorial service took place at the chapel of the Wuhu General Hospital. The chapel was crowded with representatives of the Chinese government, of American and other consular offices, and of all the local Christian organizations, both Chinese and foreign. Following the service, John and Betty's remains were buried in Wuhu's lovely foreign cemetery.

Charles and Clara Scott held a "Triumph Service" in their home in Tsinan for local acquaintances who had known Betty and John. A large memorial service was held at the Star of Hope Mission in Paterson, New Jersey, for the many friends and supporters of the Stams. When the mission's auditorium, with its more than six hundred seats, was filled to overflowing, a loudspeaker was hooked up in a church across the street to accommodate all those who had come to hear the service.

At the close of the memorial service held at the Moody Bible Institute, some seven hundred students stood to their feet to signify their willingness to consecrate their lives to missionary service wherever the Lord might lead them. Another two hundred students at Wheaton College similarly dedicated themselves to Christ's service.

Students from Betty's alma mater, Wilson College, wrote to report that the memorial service held there was the most spiritually impressive ceremony they had ever witnessed. The college's president, Dr. Warfield, had been bedridden for weeks with illness but rallied his strength to give the memorial address himself.

The governing board of Wilson announced the adoption of Helen Priscilla as "The College Baby," pledging that the entire cost of her higher education at that institution would be completely underwritten. Wilson students also took up a voluntary collection of one hundred dollars, which they mailed to China to help supply Helen's immediate needs.

Around the world came gifts for The Miracle Baby. A number of couples volunteered to adopt Helen, but Charles and Clara Scott chose to assume that responsibility themselves. After growing up in her grandparents' home, Helen eventually married and had children of her own. She has lived with her family in the United States but has chosen to conceal her childhood identity and her present whereabouts.

John and Betty's willingness to lay down their lives in the service of Christ challenged and inspired thousands of other believers, literally around the world, to serve Him with greater consecration and courage. Betty's brother Francis, who was studying at Princeton Seminary at the time of her death, wrote to his parents: "I know, if your experience has been at all like mine, that this wicked deed has jolted us powerfully out of the spiritual lethargy into which we had slipped, and that even though we thought we were giving our best, it wasn't enough and lacked the depth of consecration and the power of witness that we ought to have as God's ambassadors to men."[5]

Betty's sister Helen testified of the increased desire which she and her husband, George Gordon Mahy, had

198

to go to China as missionaries after the death of their loved ones: "We were still awaiting the decisions of our board regarding our appointment when the news was flashed to us of the cruel martyrdom of my sister and her husband by Communist bandits. This brutal slaying only intensified our convictions.

"The Stephen-like fearlessness and peace of the beloved martyrs, the unflinching loyalty of Pastor Lo and many other Chinese Christians, even at the peril of their lives, all showed up so powerfully against the almost incredible brutality of the Communist forces that it would seem impossible the whole world could remain blind to the issues. Our desire to be sent to China then became so strong as to be painful. Every other consideration became secondary, for never did a country present itself in a needier light, and never could witness be made in a more strategic place than in China now, as she stands at the parting of the ways."[6]

A friend of Betty's who was first influenced toward service in China by her during their student days at Wilson College had since made application with the CIM. Following the deaths of Betty and John, a CIM official wrote to the candidate to test her reaction to current conditions in China. The young woman responded, "I do not fear death, but would be happy to die in China or here for Christ's cause. The chief desire would be that my death should be a means of leading precious souls to Christ. Being human, I naturally dread suffering and distress of body, and abuse at the hands of wicked men. But I really believe that I have faced all these possibilities and counted the cost. This tragic and terrible happening does not frighten me but, rather, makes me regird myself with the armor of God."[7]

John and Betty's deaths also allowed a powerful Christian testimony to be borne on a large scale to the unbelieving world. The front pages of hundreds of secular newspapers scattered around the globe carried the story of their murder in China, along with long accounts of their faith and dedication. The printed reports of their service and testimony were used of God to play a part in drawing some to salvation. Among this number was a Hindu gentleman who, after reading of their martyrdom, became a firm believer in the Lord Jesus and a zealous witness for Him.

The February 1935 issue of the CIM's official publication, *China's Millions*, included a lengthy tribute to the mission organization's seventy-third and seventy-fourth martyrs. The tribute closed with these fitting words:

> *It has been a long time since any event connected with the mission fields has made so wide and profound an impression in this country. We believe that John and Betty Stam may by their death have spoken even more loudly than by their brief lives of devoted service. Let no one call this ending of their earthly career a tragedy, for in reality it is a triumph.*
>
> *It recalls to our mind the old seal of the noble Moravian Brotherhood consisting of a lamb upon a crimson background, together with the cross of resurrection and a banner of victory. Underneath all was the motto in Latin which, translated into English, reads: OUR LAMB HAS CONQUERED; LET US FOLLOW HIM. John and Betty Stam were true followers of the Lamb—in life, and even unto death. Again the challenge comes: "Who follows in their train?"[8]*

# Endnotes

**Chapter 1**

1. The dialogue and chain of events described in this chapter are based on the depositions that Mei Tsong-fuh and Li Ming-chin made before George Atcheson Jr., Consul of the United States of America, in and for the consular district of Nanking, China, on January 1, 1935, as found in Collection 449: Ephemera of John Cornelius and Elisabeth Alden (Scott) Stam, 1923–1940; n.d., Archives of the Billy Graham Center, Wheaton, Illinois (hereafter cited as Stam Documents). Used by permission.
2. John Stam to CIM officials, December 6, 1934, Stam Documents.

**Chapter 4**

1. Mary Geraldine Taylor, *The Triumph of John and Betty Stam* (Chicago: Moody, 1935), p. 33. Used by permission of OMF International.
2. Ibid., pp. 34–36.
3. Ibid., pp. 38–39.
4. Ibid., p. 37.

**Chapter 5**

1. Taylor, *The Triumph*, pp. 46–47.
2. Lee S. Huizenga, *John and Betty Stam: Martyrs* (Grand Rapids: Zondervan, 1935), p. 64.
3. Taylor, *The Triumph*, p. 51.
4. Ibid., p. 52.
5. Ibid., p. 52–53.

**Chapter 6**

1. Taylor, *The Triumph*, p. 21.
2. Ibid., pp. 73–74.
3. Ibid., p. 29.
4. Ibid.
5. Ibid., p. 30.
6. E. Schuyler English, *By Life and by Death, Excerpts and Lessons from the Diary of John C. Stam* (Grand Rapids: Zondervan, 1938), p. 27.
7. Ibid., p. 34.
8. Ibid., p. 54.

## Chapter 7

1. Taylor, *The Triumph*, pp. 57–58.
2. Ibid., p. 63–64.
3. English, *By Life*, p. 20.

## Chapter 8

1. English, *By Life*, p. 36.
2. Taylor, *The Triumph*, p. 26.
3. Ibid., p. 24
4. Lee S. Huizenga, *John and Betty Stam: Martyrs* (Grand Rapids: Zondervan, 1935), pp. 46–47.
5. John Stam to his parents, September 23, 1931, Stam Documents.
6. English, *By Life*, p. 37.
7. John Stam's Moody graduation speech, April 21, 1932, Stam Documents.

## Chapter 9

1. Stam diary, June 30, 1932, Stam Documents.
2. Stam diary, September 22, 1932, Stam Documents.
3. John Stam to his parents, September 24, 1932, Stam Documents.
4. Taylor, *The Triumph*, p. 75.

## Chapter 10

1. John Stam to his family members, October 13, 1932, Stam Documents.
2. Stam diary, October 12, 1932, Stam Documents.
3. John Stam to his family members, October 19, 1932, Stam Documents.

## Chapter 11

1. John Stam to his family members, October 26, 1932, Stam Documents.
2. Stam diary, November 3, 1932, Stam Documents.
3. John Stam to his family members, November 12, 1932, Stam Documents.
4. John Stam to his family members, November 5, 1932, Stam Documents.
5. Stam diary, December 3, 1932; December 11, 1932; December 17, 1932; January 8, 1933; March 4, 1933; March 11, 1933; Stam Documents.

6. Stam diary, October 28, 1932; November 2, 1932; November 4, 1932; November 12, 1932; December 14, 1932; Stam Documents.

## Chapter 12
1. Taylor, *The Triumph*, p. 83.
2. Ibid., pp. 85–87.

## Chapter 13
1. Taylor, *The Triumph*, p. 88.
2. Betty Scott to John Stam, December 11, 1932, Stam Documents.
3. John Stam to his family members, December 24, 1932, Stam Documents.

## Chapter 14
1. Stam diary, December 30, 1932, Stam Documents.
2. John Stam to his family members, January 14, 1933, Stam Documents.
3. Stam diary, January 15, 1933, Stam Documents.
4. John Stam to his family members, December 17, 1932, Stam Documents.
5. John Stam to his family members, December 10, 1932, Stam Documents.
6. Stam diary, January 17, 1933, Stam Documents.
7. John Stam to his family members, February 4, 1933, Stam Documents.
8. Betty Scott to John Stam's parents, January 24, 1933, Stam Documents.
9. Betty Scott to John Stam, n.d., Stam Documents.
10. Stam diary, February 21, 1933, Stam Documents.

## Chapter 15
1. John Stam to his family members, March 4, 1933, Stam Documents.
2. John Stam to his family members, March 18, 1933, Stam Documents.
3. John Stam to his family members, March 25, 1933, Stam Documents.
4. John Stam to his family members, March 29, 1933, Stam Documents.
5. Taylor, *The Triumph*, pp. 94–95.

6. John Stam to his family members, April 22, 1933, Stam Documents.

7. Taylor, *The Triumph*, pp. 96–97.

8. John Stam to his family members, May 15, 1933, Stam Documents.

## Chapter 16

1. John Stam to his supporters, June 1, 1933, Stam Documents.

2. Ibid.

3. John Stam to his family members, May 29, 1933, Stam Documents.

4. Taylor, *The Triumph*, p. 97.

5. John Stam to his family members, May 29, 1933, Stam Documents.

## Chapter 17

1. John Stam to his family members, July 1, 1933, Stam Documents.

2. John Stam to his family members, July 10, 1933, Stam Documents.

3. Stam diary, August 4, 1933, Stam Documents.

4. John Stam to his family members, August 12, 1933, Stam Documents.

5. John Stam to his family members, July 15, 1933, Stam Documents.

6. John Stam to his family members, August 12, 1933, Stam Documents.

7. Ibid.

8. John Stam to his family members, August 28, 1933, Stam Documents.

## Chapter 18

1. John Stam to his family members, September 9, 1933, Stam Documents.

2. Stam diary, September 1, 1933, September 4, 1933, Stam Documents.

3. John Stam to his family members, October 2, 1933, Stam Documents.

4. Stam diary, October 11, 1933, Stam Documents.

5. John Stam to his family members, October 15, 1933, Stam Documents.

## Chapter 19

1. Stam diary, October 16, 1933; John Stam to his family members October 31, 1933, Stam Documents.
2. John Stam to his family members, October 31, 1933, Stam Documents.
3. Charles and Clara Scott to their supporters, November 11, 1933, Stam Documents.
4. John Stam to his family members, October 27, 1933, Stam Documents.
5. John Stam to his family members, October 31, 1933, Stam Documents.
6. Stam diary, November 9, 1933, Stam Documents.
7. Stam diary, November 17, 1933, Stam Documents.

## Chapter 20

1. John Stam to his family members, November 22, 1933, Stam Documents.
2. Betty Stam to John Stam's parents, December 10, 1933, Stam Documents.
3. John Stam to his family members, December 9, 1933, Stam Documents.
4. Taylor, *The Triumph*, p. 108.
5. Betty Stam to John Stam's parents, February 16, 1934, Stam Documents.
6. John Stam to his family members, March 5, 1934, Stam Documents.
7. Ibid.

## Chapter 21

1. Betty Stam to John Stam's parents, March 28, 1934, Stam Documents.
2. John Stam to his family members, April 2, 1934, Stam Documents.
3. John Stam to his supporters, August 13, 1934, Stam Documents.
4. John Stam to his family members, June 1, 1934, Stam Documents.
5. John Stam to his family members, June 6, 1934, Stam Documents.
6. John Stam to his family members, June 18, 1934, Stam Documents.

7. Ibid.
8. John Stam to his supporters, August 13, 1934, Stam Documents.

## Chapter 22

1. John Stam to his family members, July 18, 1934, Stam Documents.
2. John Stam to his family members, August 2, 1934, Stam Documents.
3. John Stam to his family members, July 10, 1934, Stam Documents.
4. John Stam to his family members, September 8, 1934, Stam Documents.
5. Betty Stam to John Stam's parents, October 22, 1934, Stam Documents.
6. John Stam to his family members, November 19, 1934, Stam Documents.

## Chapter 23

1. John Stam to his family members, December 5, 1934, Stam Documents.
2. John Stam to friends, December 5, 1934, Stam Documents.
3. John Stam to CIM officials, December 7, 1934, Stam Documents.

## Chapter 25

1. Peter Stam telegram to CIM officials, n.d., Stam Documents.
2. Peter Stam to friends, n.d., Stam Documents.
3. Clara Scott to CIM officials, December 15, 1934, Stam Documents.
4. Peter Stam to friends, n.d., Stam Documents.
5. Taylor, *The Triumph*, p. 153.
6. Huizenga, *Martyrs*, pp. 101–02.
7. "His Witnesses Unto Death, A Tribute to John and Elisabeth Stam," *China's Millions* (February, 1935), p. 25, Stam Documents.
8. Ibid.

# Further Reading

English, E. Schuyler. *By Life and by Death, Excerpts and Lessons from the Diary of John C. Stam*. Grand Rapids: Zondervan, 1938.

Huizenga, Lee S. *John and Betty Stam: Martyrs*. Grand Rapids: Zondervan, 1935.

Taylor, Mary Geraldine. *The Triumph of John and Betty Stam*. Chicago: Moody, 1935.

White, Kathleen. *John and Betty Stam*. Minneapolis: Bethany, 1989.

Woodbridge, John D., Editor. *Ambassadors for Christ*. Chicago: Moody, 1994. Will Norton Sr., "John and Betty Stam, Triumph in Death," pp. 185–91.

Collection 449: Ephemera of John Cornelius and Elisabeth Alden (Scott) Stam, 1923–1940; n.d., Archives of the Billy Graham Center, Wheaton, Illinois. The user-friendly BGC archive contains much fascinating original source material on the Stams, including prayer letters, a diary, eyewitness accounts, photographs, and more.